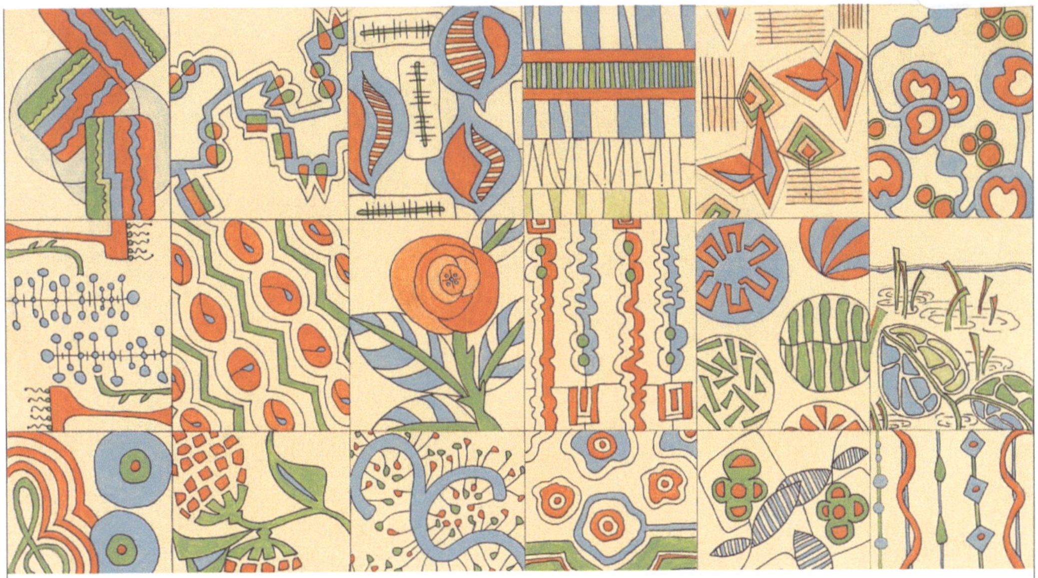

TENDING TO MY WOUNDS

Coping with Grief One Square at a Time

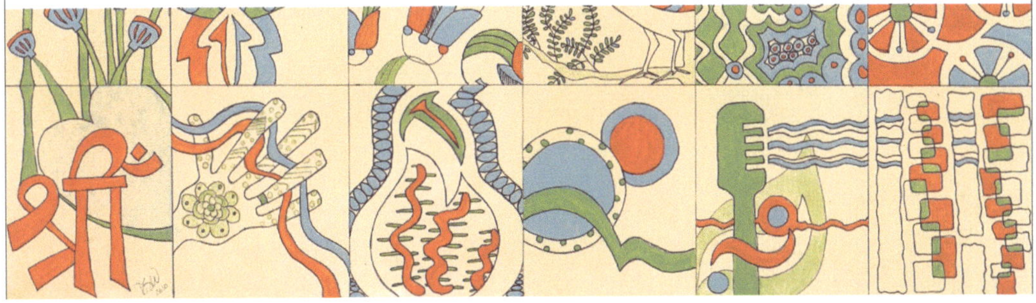

Debra Smelik Walling

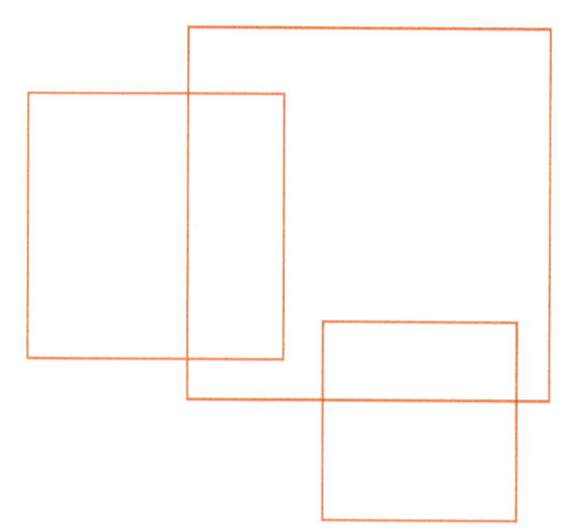

Do not surrender your grief so quickly.
Let it cut more deeply.
Let it ferment and season you.
As few human or divine ingredients can.

Hafiz of Persia

ISBN978-0-9962010-4-9

 Images of the Project SaD art canvases in this book photographed by Brian James, Brain James Gallery in St. Petersburg, Florida. Art canvases are available for licensing / production. Visit author's website at www.dswalling.com

 Every reasonable effort has been made to quote exactly as intended by its creator. Any omissions are inadvertent and will be happy to make any necessary changes to future printings.

TENDING TO MY WOUNDS

Coping with Grief One Square at a Time

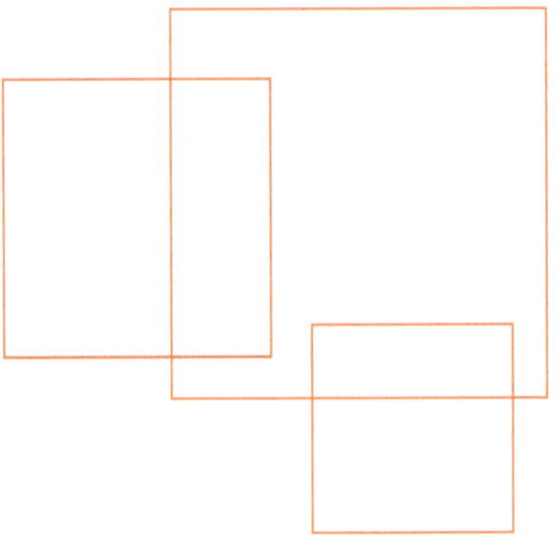

Debra Smelik Walling

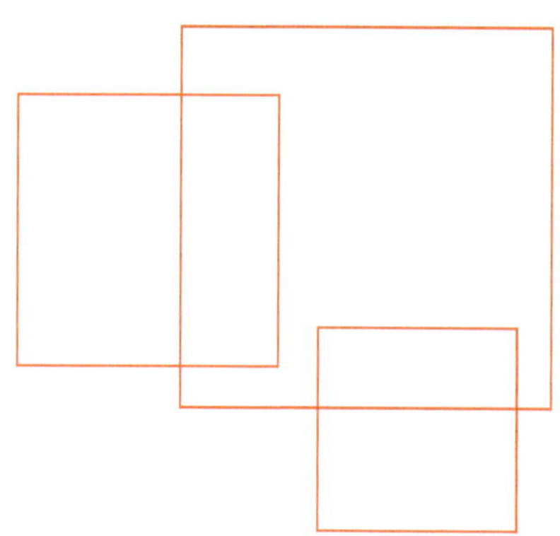

TABLE OF CONTENTS

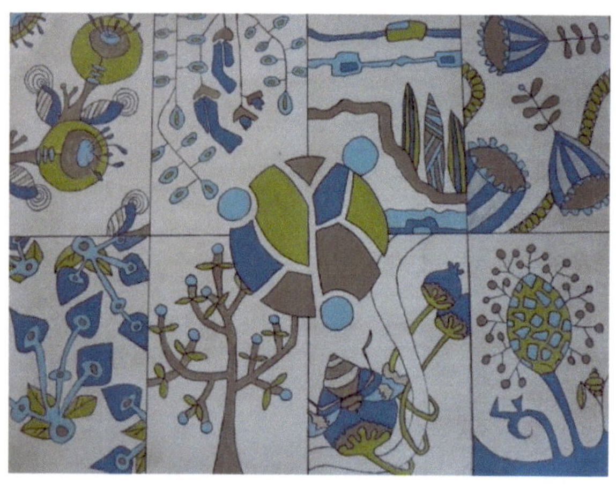

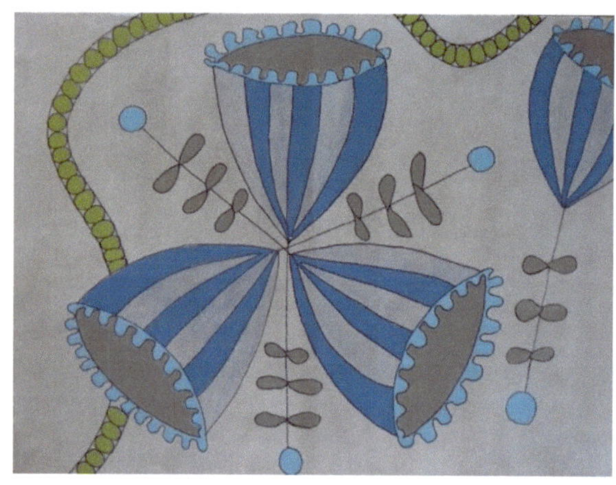

NO 24 : June 2011

IN LOVING MEMORY

of my mother

Irene Wroblewski Smelik
1926 to 2007

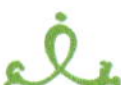

Grief is not a disorder, a disease or a sign of weakness.
It is an emotional, physical and spiritual necessity,
the price you pay for love.
The only cure for grief
is to grieve.

Earl Grollman

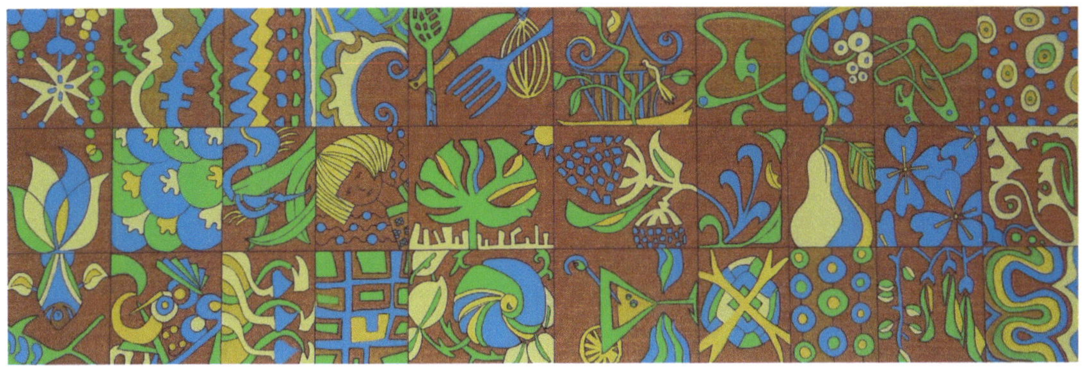

NO 43 : April 2015

FOREWORD

Encountering Debra Walling for the first time was an olfactory experience. Prior to her mother's death, Debra volunteered at a regional hospice and brought aromatherapy to the patients receiving palliative care. Her creativity and attention to detail provided compassion through the senses. Debra's aromatic mixtures evoked and transported, soothed and energized, comforted and consoled. Her passion and commitment to tending those in emotional, spiritual, mental, and physical pain were communicated through her blended fragrances.

Tending To My Wounds, Coping with Grief One Square at a Time employs a similar attention to detail in offering a personal and nuanced narrative of loss. Hers is an intimate story. The images are whiffs, brief scents on the air, redolent, gathered day by day, month by month over time to create layered notes of expressed feelings and insights. Crisp and clear arrangements of lines, shapes, and symbols belie the tangle and depth of her pain.

Like the scratches made by the person in solitary confinement on a makeshift calendar, her marking of the days depict a day-to-day identification of unfamiliar thoughts and feelings. The images created in monthly segments, document the "cumulative whole" of her grief over the death of her beloved mother. The narrative expressed through these monthly pictures draws the reader into a landscape of grief. The fragments of memories and shifting emotions found in this landscape show the inherent disruption when life events result in irrevocable loss. Colors are often muted. Missing and broken parts mirror the disorientation and confusion of the grieving individual. As nothing appears or feels familiar, the journey through this landscape is exhausting. Sadness shadows the person left behind. There is a sense of being lost, alone, and hopeless.

Debra Walling however, offers hope. She has developed a way to make the time of grieving more bearable, noted, recognized, and honored. This compilation of original journal entries and richly symbolic paintings is an extraordinary example of using art to heal. Her images represent an authentic striving for wholeness and relief. Creating order out of the chaos of grief, her innovative approach serves as a recommendation to reclaim life, harmony, and health.

Although the approach might be perceived as regimented and disciplined, structure and daily practice can be pivotal in recovery from loss. The images record the incremental steps necessary in facing change and feeling pain. Limiting the activity of self-expression to at least five, but not more than fifteen minutes per day, the task is deliberate and attainable. The technique is a measured approach to managing grief. Her work gives evidence of the length of actual and psychic time grief demands for completion.

This deliberate daily practice can bring the grieving person into the present. The action of creating an image in a small space within a prescribed time limit scaffolds effortful movement toward a goal. With a focus on the immediate, the individual can be empowered by an attainable goal. Being in the present provides respite from the pain of loss and allows formation of new coping skills. In the present, the grieving person resides in the paradox of acknowledging pain and recognizing the good things remaining in life. This action of holding two different viewpoints occupying the same space can prompt deeper reflection and potential healing.

At the time Debra began this self-directed task, I was completing a Master of Arts in Art Therapy degree. Her sensibility and focus, her dedication to using art in a therapeutic way inspired me and supported my understanding of the benefits of the art making process to address loss, ease pain, and find resolution. Regardless of the ongoing work to decipher the riddles that are contained in the images, her work demonstrates the importance of expressing the emotions that burden the grieving person. Viewing her initial exhibition and revisiting the 19 canvases over time, confirms the value and benefit of using images to tell a story. Her potent combination of journaling and painting amplifies her singular experience in dealing with grief while telling a familiar story experienced by many.

What once began as a measure to bring closure to her grief continues today as a habit. Her originality of purpose, her consistency in completing her self-directed task, and her courage to share her artistic approach and process with others remains exceptional. Permitting and welcoming others to share in her journey, she stands at the entrance to guide and support the creative endeavors of the grieving individual.

Kathleen Sullivan, MAAT, ATR-BC,
Tarpon Springs, Florida

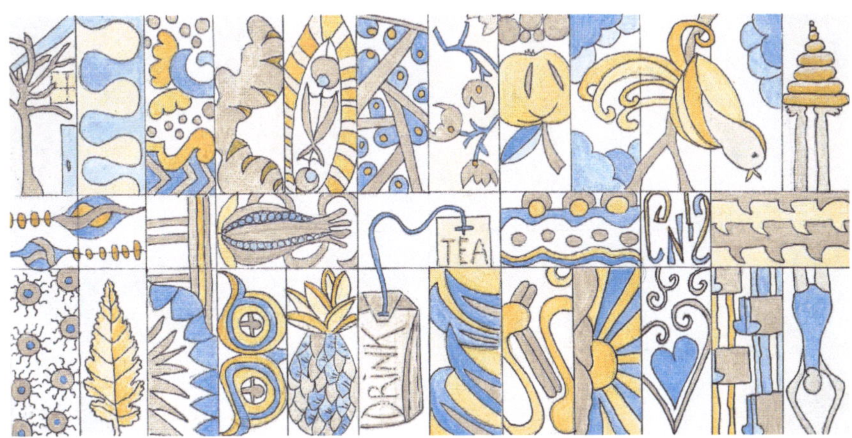

NO 37 : June 2014

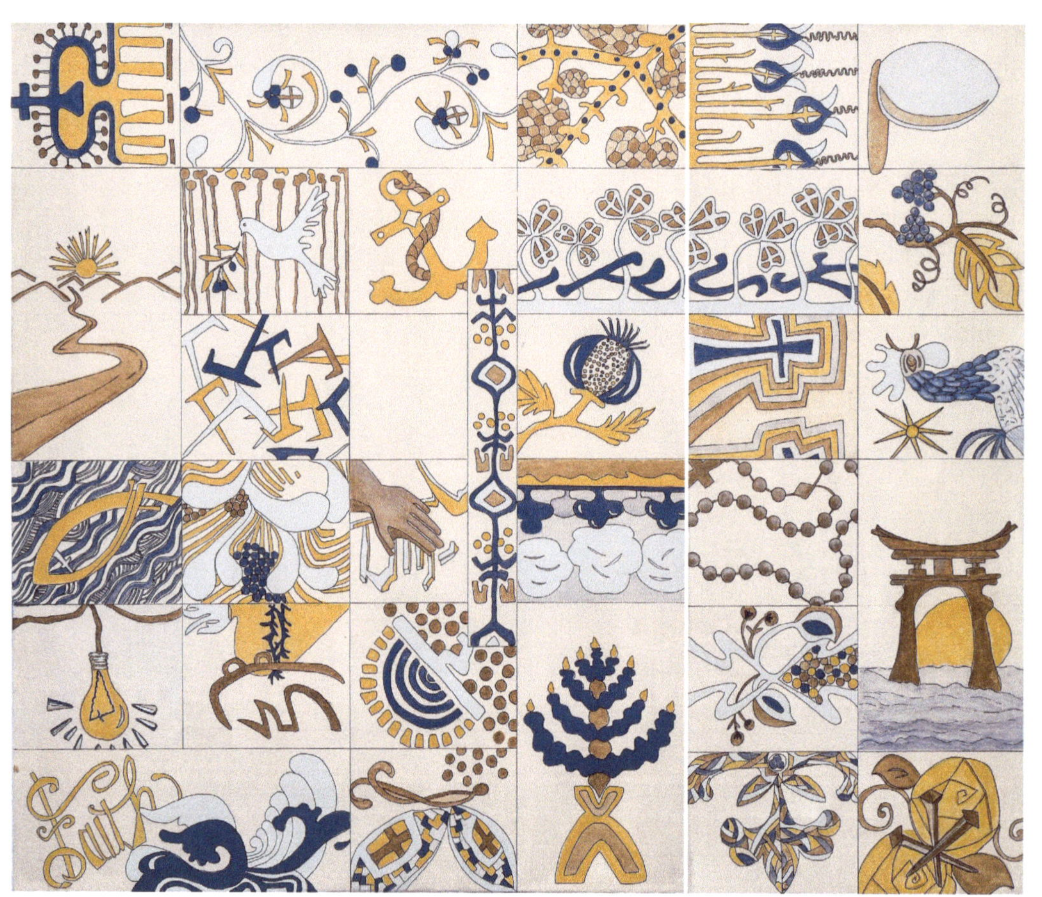

NO 38, 39 : July 2014

ACKNOWLEDGEMENTS

Heartfelt gratitude and appreciation to my husband, Jeffrey for his encouragement and who lovingly provides the tools I need to create. Thank you Dr. Patrick Sullivan, DOM and Kathleen Sullivan, MAAT, ATR-BC for taking notice of my grief, suggesting an alternative outlet of expression with encouraged interest and how the activity of a Square-a-Day (Project SaD) evolved. Appreciation to Kathleen Sullivan and Heidi Bardi for your literary review, advice and guidance; David Zimny for his expertise, ongoing enthusiasm and encouragement which helped me build the confidence to continue creating and fulfilling avenues for presentation. Grateful to Creative Care for including a collection of my canvases in the 2011, RX Art in Healthcare exhibit. Jeffrey, Dr. Patrick and Kathleen Sullivan, Traci Sutton, Bill Oefinger, Carolyn Smith, Craig Gatrel, John Ferguson, Sandra Shouse, Linda Lucas and Kevin Hughes — thank you for attending the exhibit, your moral support, listening and being a friend. Thanks Brian James Gallery Photography for your expertise, kindness and encouragement.

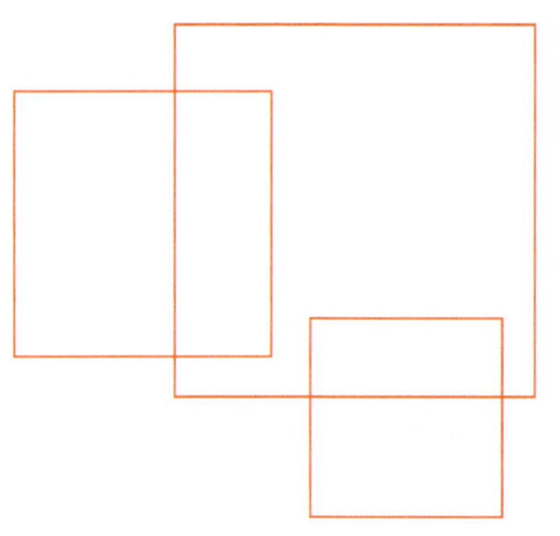

INTRODUCTION

There is a great significance to any type of loss. Loss from the death of a person or pet, loss of a job, a relationship breakup, loss of friendship, miscarriage, retirement or losing a house… the list goes on. Each type comes with grieving and mourning on some level where we become engaged in combat as the heart and soul are touched in some way, shape or form by a profound sense of sadness, disbelief and shock. Anger, guilt and fear are triggered as well as physical symptoms connected with loss.

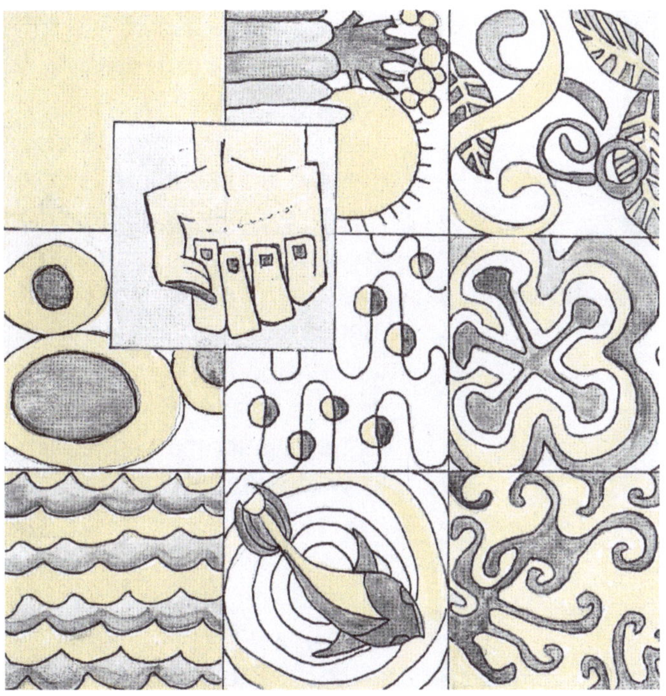

NO 32 : January 2014

The intensity varies in all of this, yet how we feel, handle and contend with the difficulties of loss is truly a distinctive and personal journey that will be expressed and experienced in ways so very different from one person to the next. We must learn to maneuver, to carefully guide ourselves and allow ourselves to embark upon the process of grief in a way that leads us to the healing and growth found in loss.

Resolution of grief is unique as each of our individual lives. What we want and need as we individually grieve may not always be readily accessible or obtainable and the reason to search for alternative sources. To help us through as we create our own haven for healing. In grief we need an outlet for expressing emotions. The outlet is personal and needs to happen.

Tending To My Wounds, Coping with Grief One Square at a Time is the afterthought to Commencement of Life After Death, the personal grief journal I created the moment our family was struck by the unknown certainties of abrupt sickness, leading to the death of our mother. The personal grief journal takes a peek into the heart and soul of my grief expressed through the written word and how I responded to my needs in sadness, healing and protection. While keeping the grief journal I wrote the first notion, usually based on my emotions, that came to my mind; giving little to no thought to any particular moment or day. I just wrote. Some made perfect sense to me at the particular time of grief in which it was expressed, therefore it helped to heal.

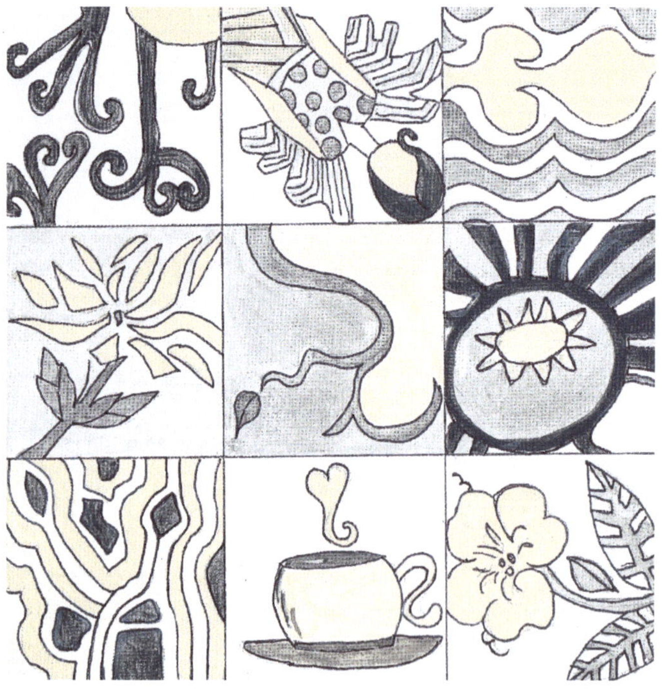

NO 33 : February 2014

The same applies to the idea behind this book. However, in Tending To My Wounds, my grief is expressed through drawing and painting, another way I explored and released the lingering sadness that shadows after death. At random, with no thought given to the mood or emotion, I just drew. A place for expression that allows for the needed time to weave through loss and to mend the broken threads. The snippets that accompany this pictorial are taken from my grief journal. Integrating the two enabled a deeper expression that lead to the closure of my grief journey.

We all have insight and perspective. We all have value. We all have experiences, joys and sorrows. This book is written for added insight to the numerous sources available for support and self-help when one grieves, mourns and bereaves. In different ways, through different forms we gain knowledge. Regardless the source to handle and contend with grief, those varying approaches are what helps us to heal.

The contents of this book is presented for potential guidance, enlightenment and motivation to individuals who might be looking for or wanting additional ways to contend with the difficulties that sometime arise as one grieves (expressing feelings, thoughts and reaction to the loss) or as one mourns (adapting to the new life without the deceased or loss experienced).

While best efforts and intentions have been used in preparing this book, each grief situation differs from one another, thus the strategies and outcome expressed might not be suitable for other specific situations. Either way it is hoped that the process might find use where applicable and that the art can be celebrated.

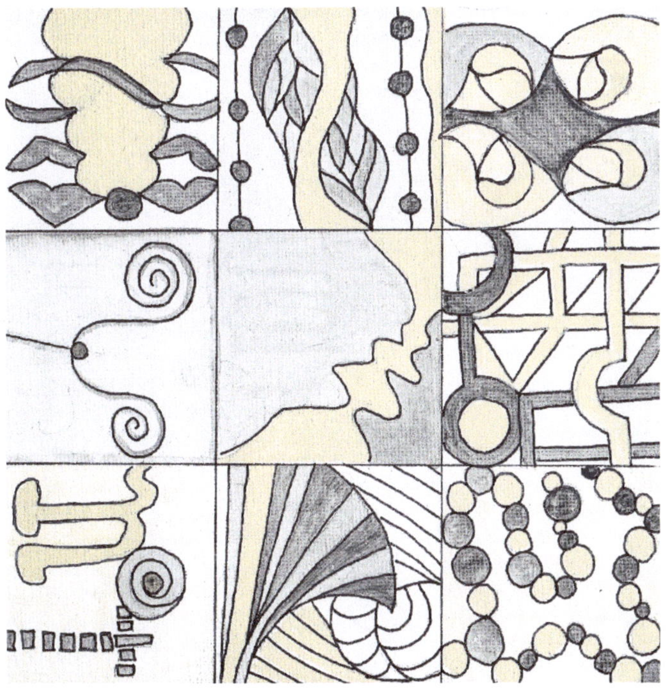

NO 34 : March 2014

Should you have the interest to tap into a different realm of grief healing, may Tending to My Wounds, Coping with Grief One Square at a Time be a muse or guide as you or someone you know journeys through the process of grief and mourning.

Debra Smelik Walling
St. Petersburg, Florida

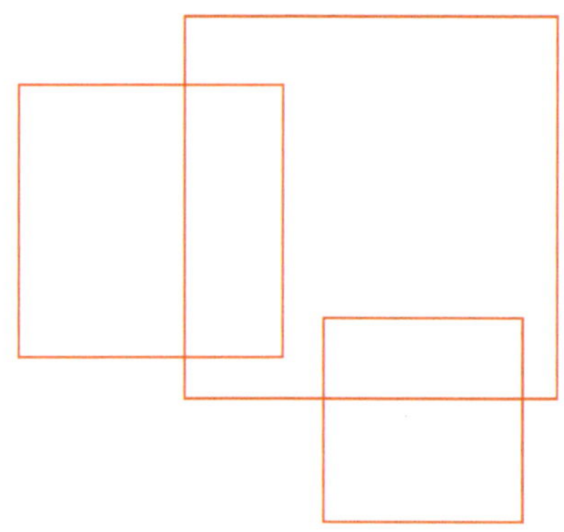

Written after my mother's funeral, when I was alone and silence was my only comfort.

SOUGHT SOLACE

Attainment unforeseen
new day, every day
life with a void
how do I survive?

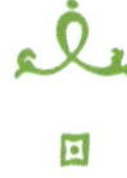

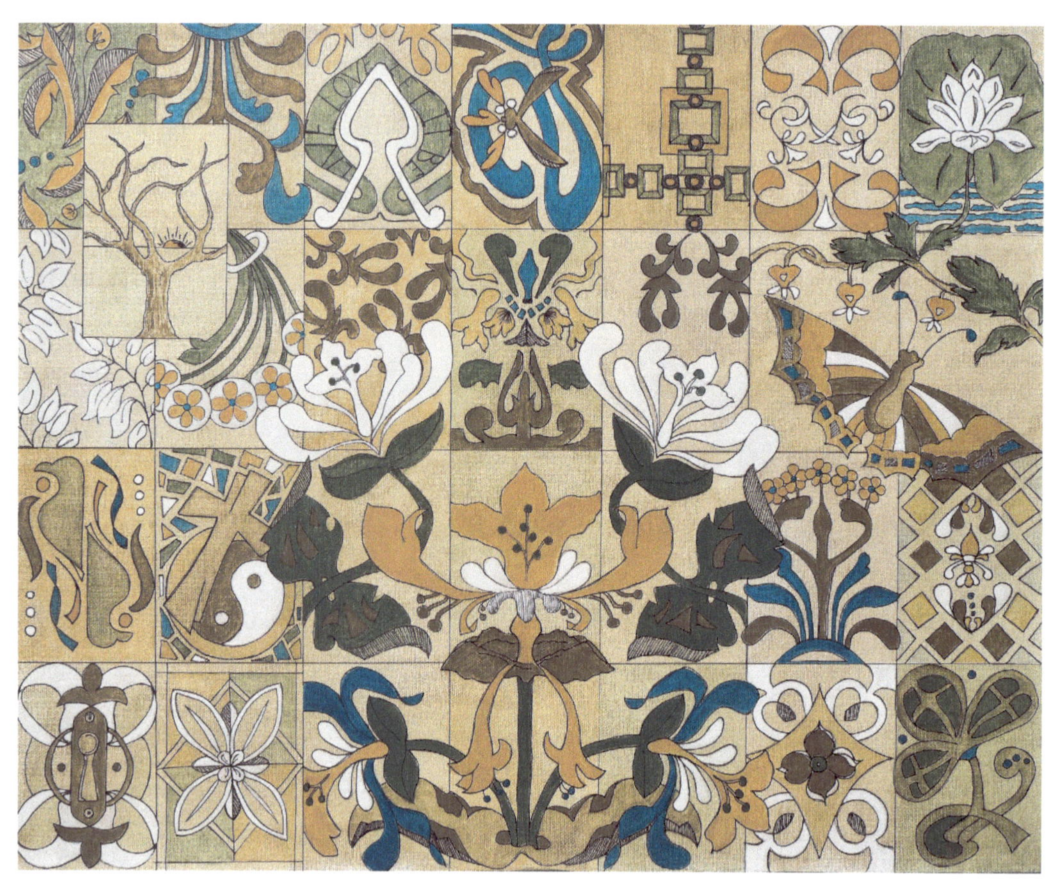

NO 01 : February 2008

TENDING TO MY WOUNDS

After the tender expressions of sympathy from family and friends ended it was time to face the bleak and dismal emptiness that was about to shadow my world. Namely the process of grief, the commencement of my life after my mother's death. Despite my own preparedness and trusting God is with me every step of the way, still the cloud of great sadness restricts. Difficult to move forward, to get involved with the world around me and energy is limited. Tending to the simplest of tasks is toilsome despite seeking comforts in the methods and forms available.

I made the decision to let grief follow me wherever I go and allow it the time it needs. I will not fight it nor will I ignore it. While I do not like the way it makes me feel, nor do I care for the pain it causes, I refuse to tolerate the bitterness. I will allow nothing to interfere with the love and the memories of my mother. I grieve, I mourn her death in spite of the deluge of tears and the loneliness or multitude of mixed emotions that creep up unexpectedly. After all, it is the memories both good and bad that will be my major comfort during the grieving process. The gremlin of grief does not reign. My love reigns.

Beyond support groups, self-help books, conversations and prayer it is through the written word that I find the most comfort in contending with grief's difficulties, dealing with and understanding death. Yet no matter how many avenues I explore, the void remains and the path to healing continues.

Then one day, I lay quietly and comfortably at the White Crane Clinic as the tranquil music softly permeates the room. During an acupuncture treatment Dr. Patrick Sullivan, DOM asks the simple questions, "How have you been?" "How are you feeling since the loss of your mother?" It has been six months since anyone made inquiry into how I am feeling. Yet Dr. Sullivan, remembered.

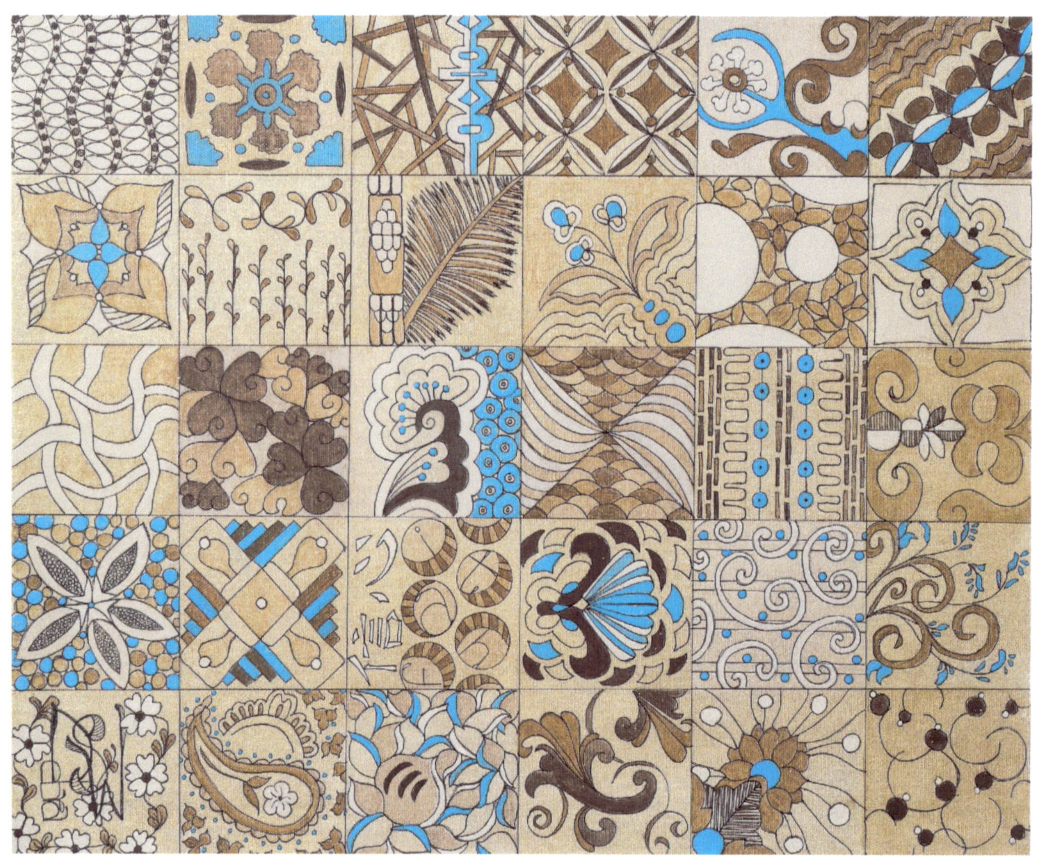

NO 02 : April 2008

Dr. Sullivan listens as I continue to share my woes of grief. He is aware of a certain sadness my drive to his office initiates. It was my mother who accompanied me to the White Crane Clinic on the morning of December 11, 2006. Havoc strikes never expecting death to take mom 31 days later. Little did I know December 11th was the last day I would hear her laughter, be intrigued by her stories or forever comforted knowing with all my faults my mom's arms would never again, embrace me in a hug. I vividly remember, when she arrived at my house earlier that particular morning. My nose tickled by the stray hairs that framed her petite face as I caught the faintest whiff of whatever powder, perfume or lotion she chose for the day blending nicely with the natural scent unique to mom; a pleasant and comforting scent I have grown accustomed to over my 51 years.

One year, one month, 25 days and little, if anything has changed. As I tend to my wounds the melancholy, the black hole of emptiness remains. I have moments where I want to vanish for I wonder if I will ever be released from the clutches of grief. Floundering I begin to doubt and question, will grief ever end or will it linger perpetually for the rest of my life. Time will tell. Family and friends seem to distance themselves and it is as if I am suddenly all alone. The mind unable to stay focused yet I continue all efforts to fight the battle by praying positive and rely on the comfort found in keeping a written grief journal.

Dr. Sullivan and I deliberate the topic of death, it leads to the topic of grief, which leads to the topic of birth and rebirth, touching on all emotions in some way or another. He spoke of support groups and self-help books and I shared my encounters with such leading to his suggestion that I consider the therapeutic value found in using art for healing as I journey through sadness from my mother's death.

The suggestion: To pick a 'canvas'. A piece of paper or an art canvas. A medium of choice, such as paint, pencil, charcoal or ink. Whichever medium I felt comfortable using. The process is straight forward. The chosen canvas is gridded into a number of squares to accommodate the number of days for the current month. Each day one square is approached for not less than five minutes and no more than fifteen minutes. Not contemplating on what will be drawn nor deciding a theme, fill one square and when the

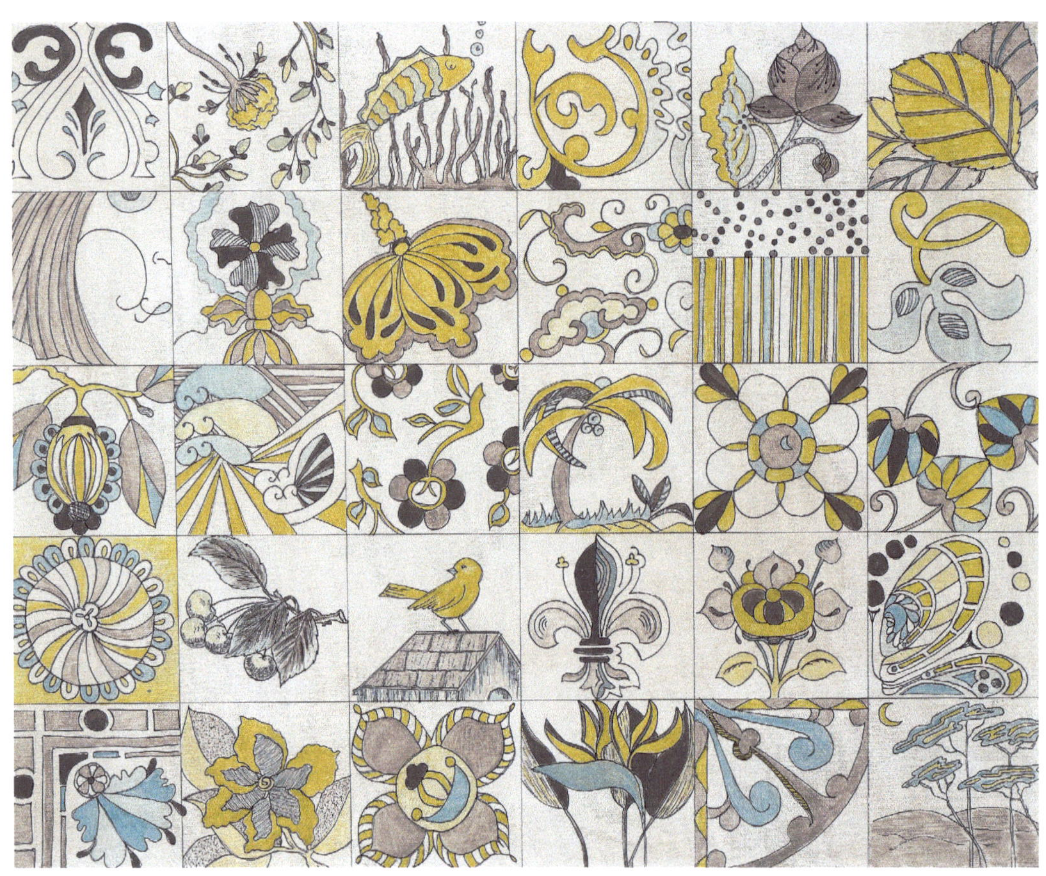

NO 04 : June 2008

time is up; stop and set the canvas aside until the following day. The idea is to simply let the medium of choice touch the canvas, allowing it to reveal one's feelings and thoughts to create a visual expression within a very short time.

When the month ends and all squares are filled, an art therapist trained to recognize nonverbal symbols and metaphors would review and evaluate this visual expression helping a client understand what would have otherwise been difficult and perhaps awkwardly written or spoken words. The feelings or thoughts being communicated in the art can therefore help one gain insight, to possibly obtain a better understanding of oneself or the relationships with others.

In my case, at the end of my healing through art adventure there would not be an art therapist. No one to review the art or help process the message held deep within this practice. For me, it was not what might be unearthed to help me resolve, reduce, achieve or manage but the importance to begin this adventure in hopes of two things. First, I thought the task and the commitment to one small square-a-day would help me relearn how to focus. Grief has a way of muddling the mind, causing behavior to surprise not only yourself but those around you. This provided the opportunity to realize it was time to quit floundering and make some type of commitment to reclaim my life. Second, the endeavor offered the possibility of another escape to a special place where I could relieve some of the grief, sadness and sorrow that blankets my soul, those unable to put into words.

I understand art therapy is about creating art, the process of self expression. A way to improve mental health and emotional well-being. In February 2008, my exploration into a visual expression of grief began. I called it Project SaD (square-a-day) with the intent to follow the process for one month, thus only one completed piece would be the result.

Now at 41 canvases later Project SaD continues. Taking a step back to look at this task I realize the impact of Dr. Sullivan's suggestion as I mourned the death of my mother. What I discovered was recovery through this somewhat meditative state engaging the visual

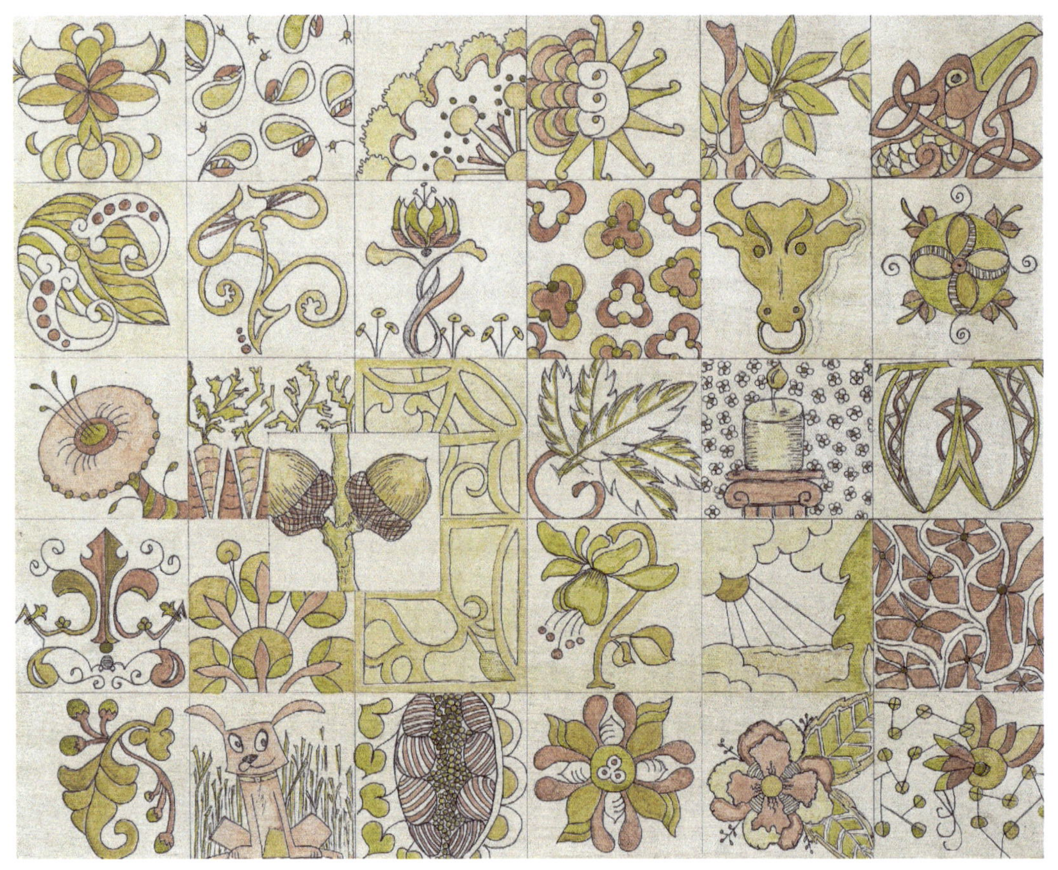

NO 05 : July 2008

journaling of my emotions. Instead of words I used shapes, color, memories and moments of the past and the present to tend to my wounded spirit, passing through the suffering to awake and return to the land of the living.

Looking for what I called The Passage, to move through, over and under the toil of sadness and grief; the passage from living life as it was with my mom to now, living life without her. Through the canvases of Project SaD I find my grief no longer speaks in tears. I find that I can face this new life of firsts. I am not as I was, the joy of life ends in grief. I will survive. My mom taught me how and joy rebounds.

As one views the canvases and reads the grief journal entries in this book, the same applies to those that read the prayers, poetry or stories that I have written. May the experience be uplifting to you as they are for me and I equally hope that you will be motivated to pick up a pen, a paint brush or whichever implement is more fitting to your desire and begin to explore the colors of your own heart.

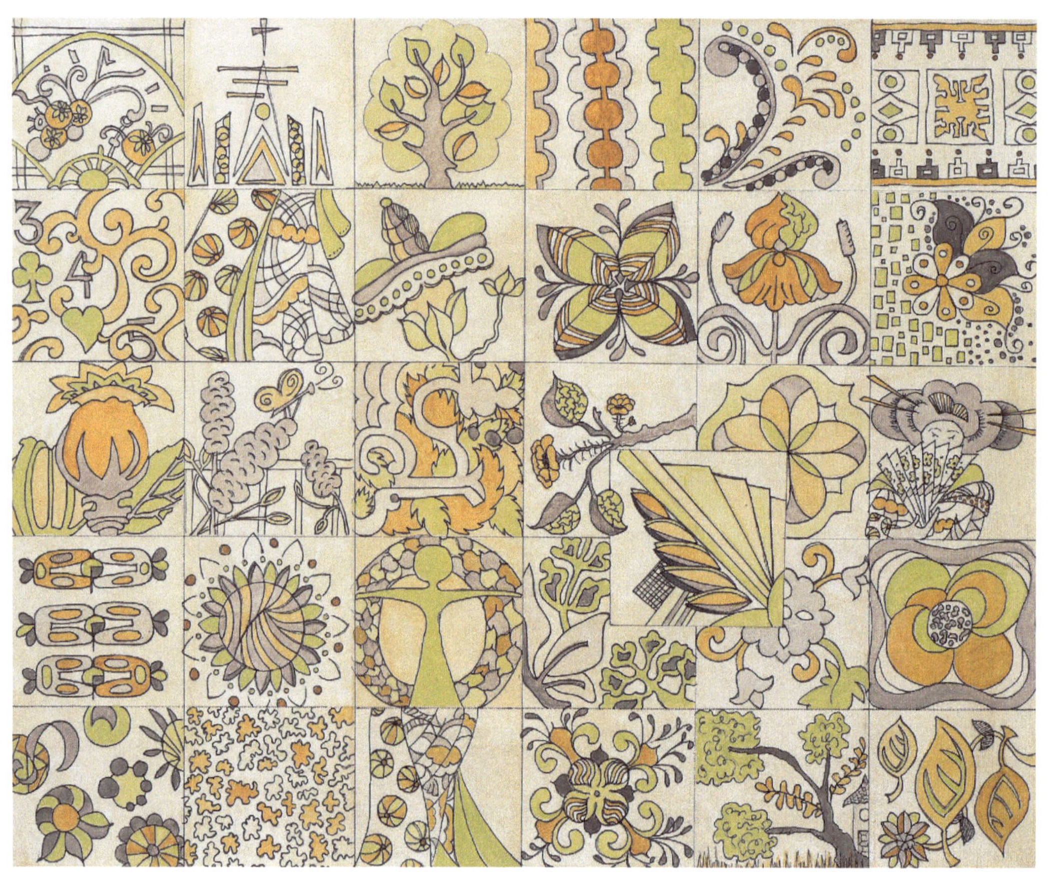

NO 06 : August 2008

THE PORTRAYAL OF MY GRIEF

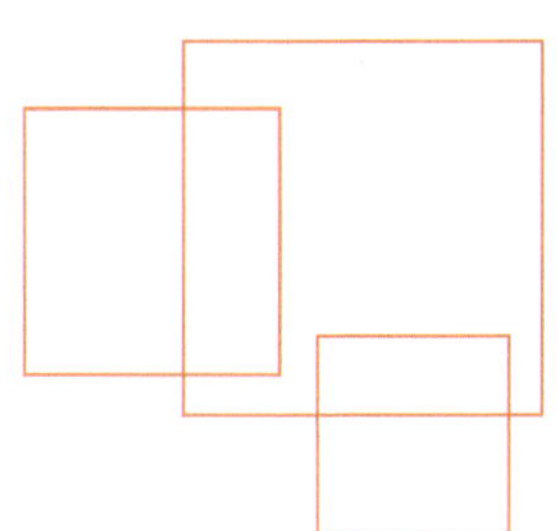

Each square reflects a moment in my day.

It can hold a memory in the making, a mood, an event, encounter or emotion.

Doodling with minimal thought, minimal time.

What I draw might reflect happiness, sorrow or another emotion.

A spot to fill, to release whatever emotion currently wraps around my heart and soul.

With hope to accept the situation in front of me or around me. To live, love and let it be.

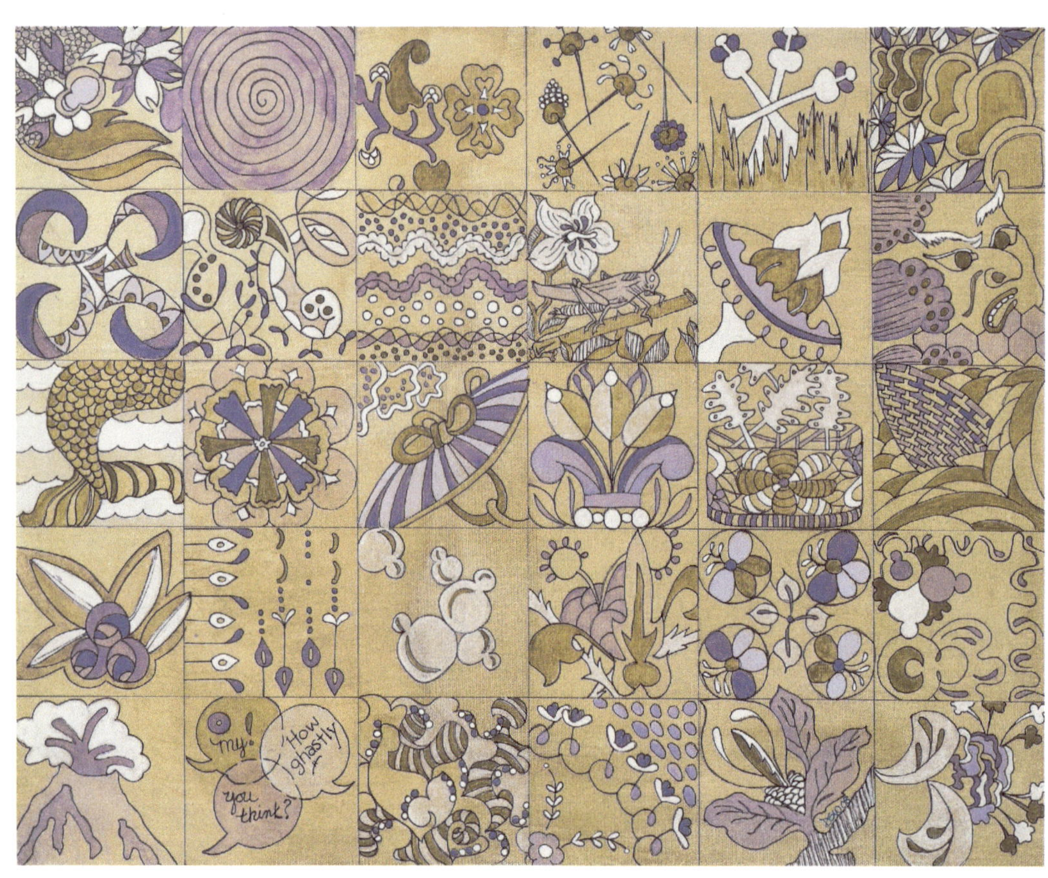

NO 07 : September 2008

SOME DAYS

Some days are good, some are not so good. Some days I shed many tears while on other days only a few as a smile attempts to emerge while I make the effort to reminisce of the before, during and the after.

On some days my inability to deal with or to understand the who, what, when, where and why of my grief is of no matter. Then on the flip side, as I try to make sense of this mere lack of absolute uncertainty, it is a major struggle. I remain aloof in this web of sadness. The words written express what I am feeling at a particular moment. It is those thoughts and my actions or reactions that are helping me to recover and reclaim my life. Tending to the simplest tasks of everyday living becomes toilsome though I persevere and tend to the responsibilities.

Some days, I know I did something or tended to someone or something, but I just could not tell you exactly or who it involved. There are times I walked around feeling lifeless and apathetic. I am aware of this behavior, but on other days I am not. If by chance our paths happened to cross on one of those days, then possibly an apology could very well be due. At times my mind has a mind of its own and I find it difficult to control in grief and mourning.

Too, I wonder, Where have my friends gone? Where has my family gone? Sometimes I feel all alone. Where did you go? There are times when I don't want to be alone, yet other times alone is all that I want. Just to be alone. For I want nothing, I feel nothing, I need nothing except to vanish from the realm.

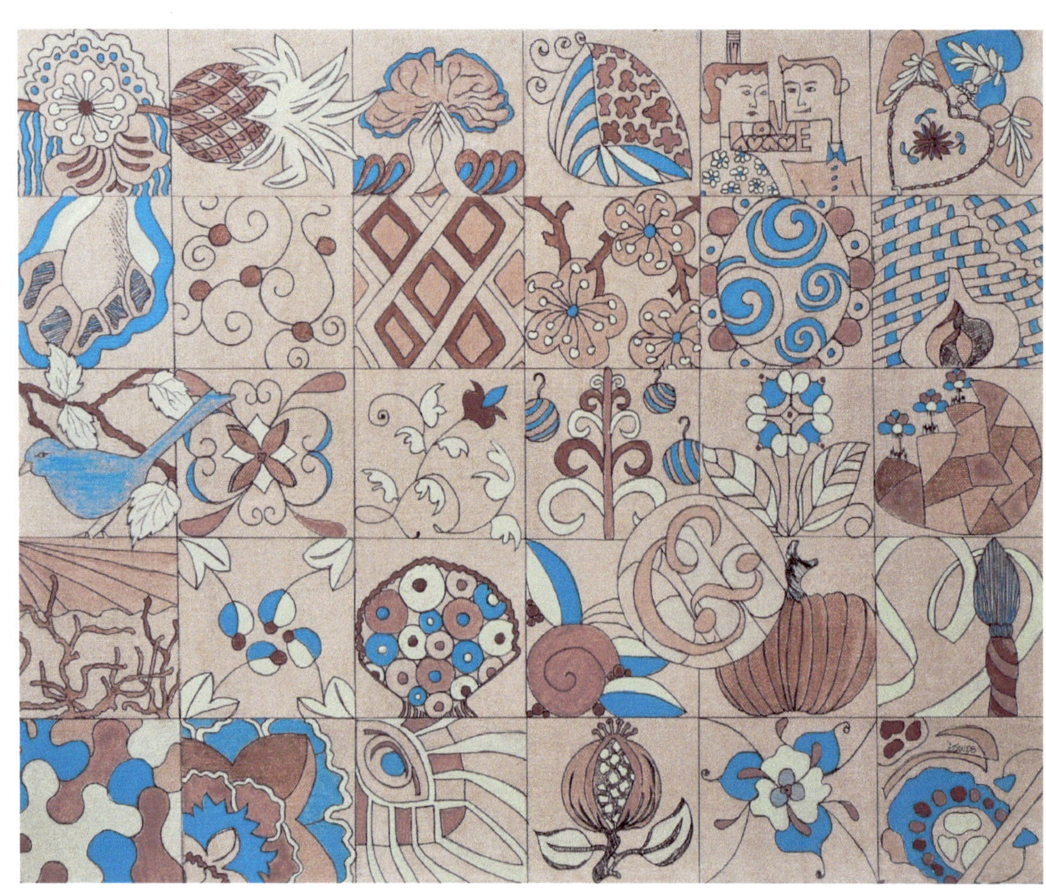

NO 08 : October 2008

Sometimes the stages or symptoms of grief hit all at once, sometimes not at all. They can loop back and forth and sometimes I am hit with a completely different set of physical, emotional and mental symptoms. I do not dismiss a single one of them, they are normal and they are expected. Although I struggle, I endure without complaint or resistance. It is the only way to heal, the only way to renew the body and soothe the soul as it was — before death.

ME, MYSELF and MY CHARACTER

headache	▪	lack of energy
inability to concentrate	▪	loneliness
don't care, why not attitude	▪	numbness
going crazy	▪	muscle tension
impaired	▪	withdrawal
despondent	▪	sense the presence of mom
difficulty in decision making	▪	cry
sadness	▪	restlessness
shock	▪	escape life that I know
lack of productivity	▪	yearning
despair	▪	emptiness

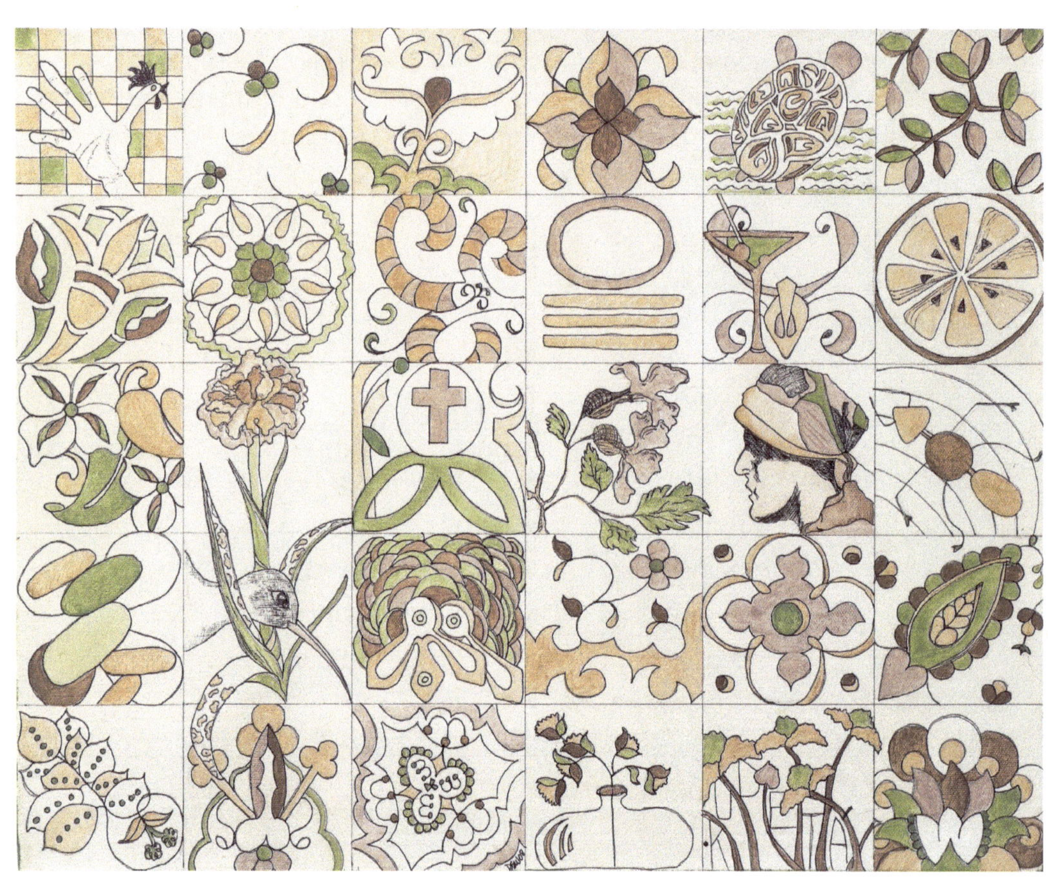

NO 09 : November 2008

POWER SURROUNDS MEMORIES

The power of sadness,
only I can delegate, mandate and nominate its intensity.
I gladly allow sadness to run its course
despite the torrent of tears.

Void surrounds my heart,
yet I can do nothing but fill that space
with the renewal of memories.

I miss you mom.

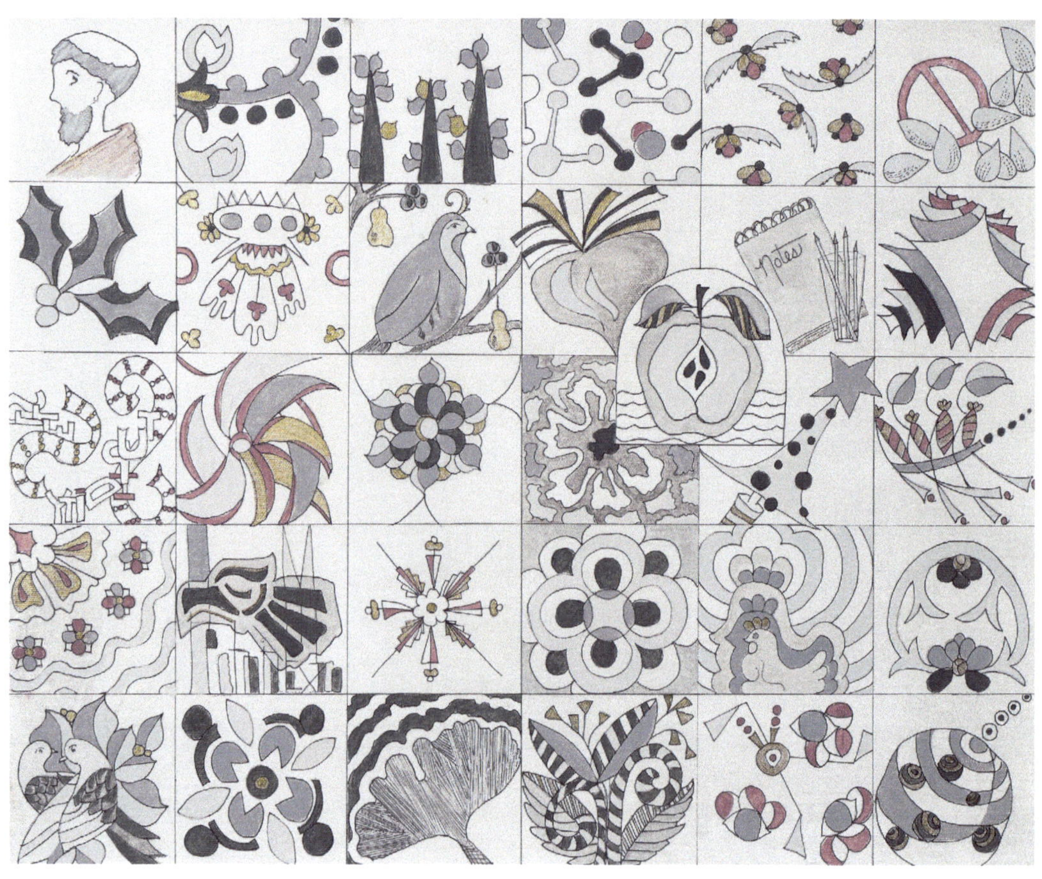

NO 10 : December 2008

GRIEF, THE SCAR

Wounded.

Grief is the pain.

Consciousness void, so it seems
or so I think.

I will heal, will I not?

The scar
to remind me of pain suffered
possibly
cultivate character

In time, to heal
I will.

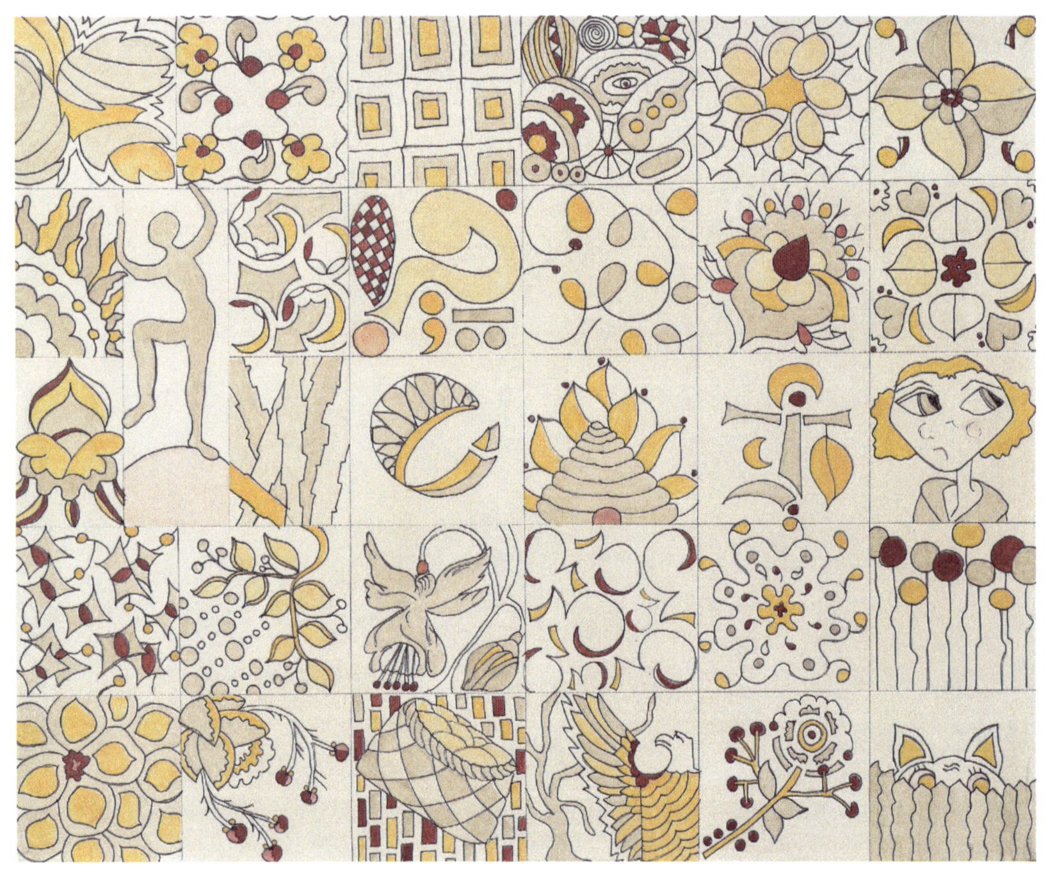

NO 11 : January 2009

Attempting to tackle the difficulty of death, boldly.

GRASP THE NETTLE

Faith empowers hope
trusting God, moving forward
possible because
death for a believer
means going home.

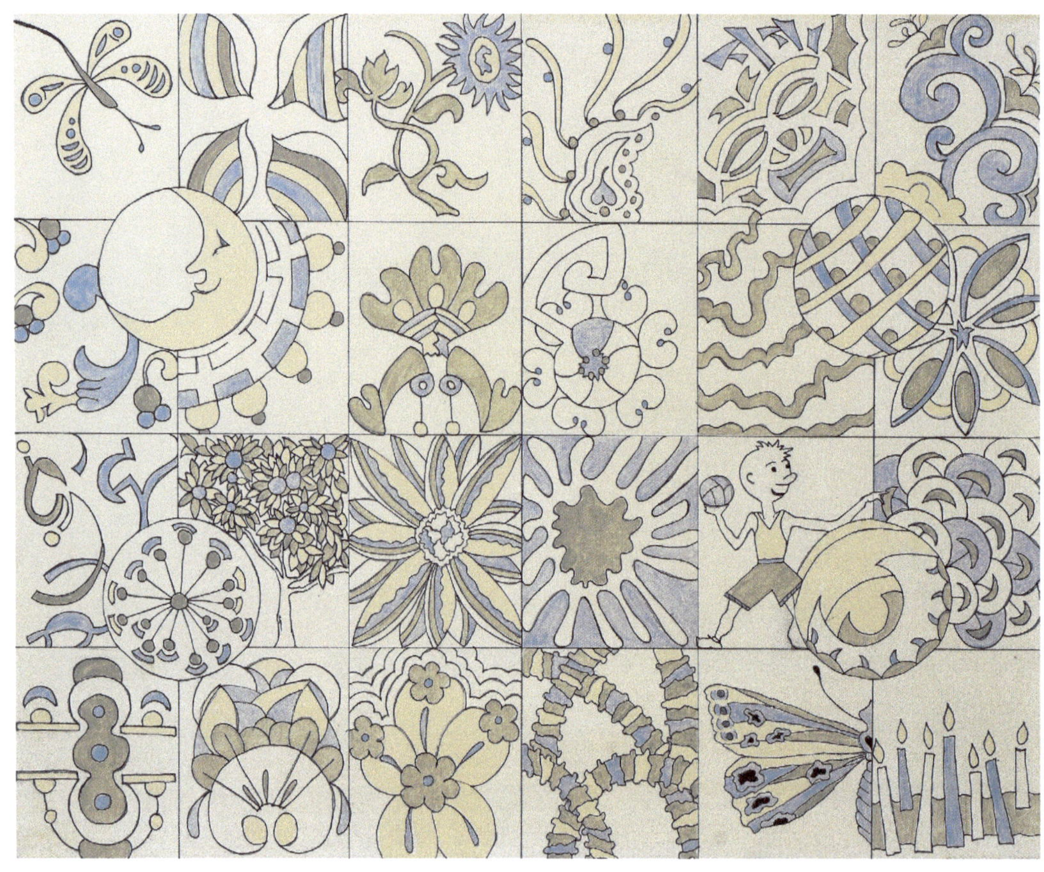

NO 12 : February 2009

Someone, somewhere. Their crisis, my crisis.
Grieve, mourn, lament, bemoan, sorrow.

IS THERE REALLY ANY DIFFERENCE?

I am heartbroken alone, I am heartbroken with others. I express orally, boldly and at times I humorously express my discontent. Sometimes I suppress while other times I regret. The variations of these nouns and verbs come with a level of energy to which we allow or choose as we experience loss. Is there really a difference when it comes to sadness?

I feel no different today at six months then I did at two months. I remain very sad that death found my mother and with the intensity of death's beginning or ending; again I question, is there really a difference when it comes to describe the power of sadness. I cry the same amount of tears with a memory as I did before death and during death as I do after death. In sadness, is there really a difference?

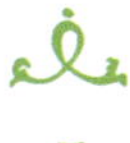

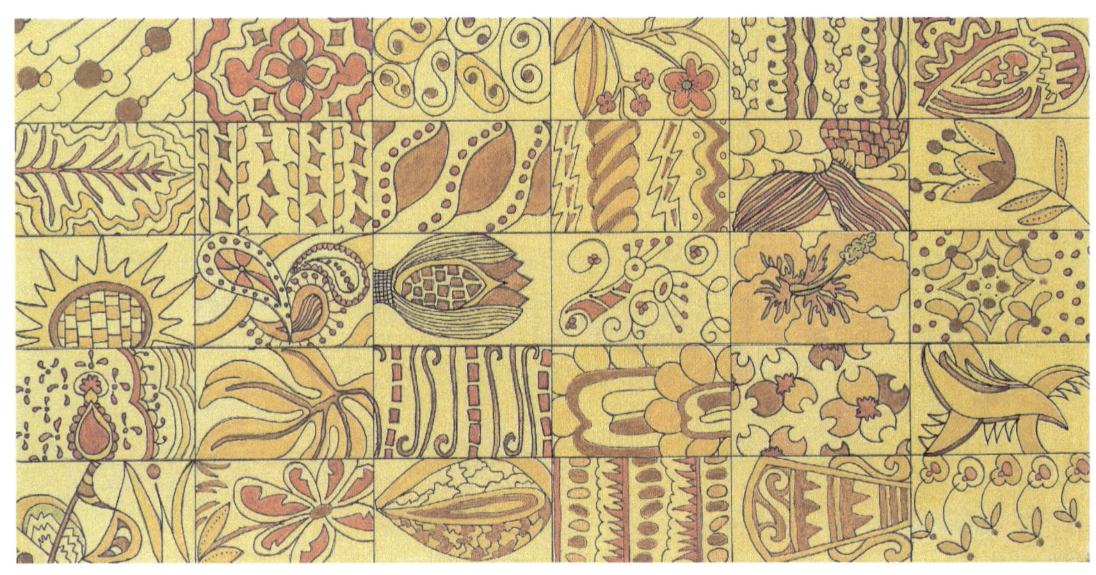

NO 13 : April 2009

GRIEF NEEDS CARE
REFUSE BITTERNESS

I will let grief follow me wherever I go, allowing it the time it needs.
I will not ignore it.
I do not like the way it makes me feel nor do I care for the pain it causes,
yet I refuse to tolerate its bitterness,
for I allow nothing to interfere with the love,
the memories of my mother
as I grieve, as I mourn.

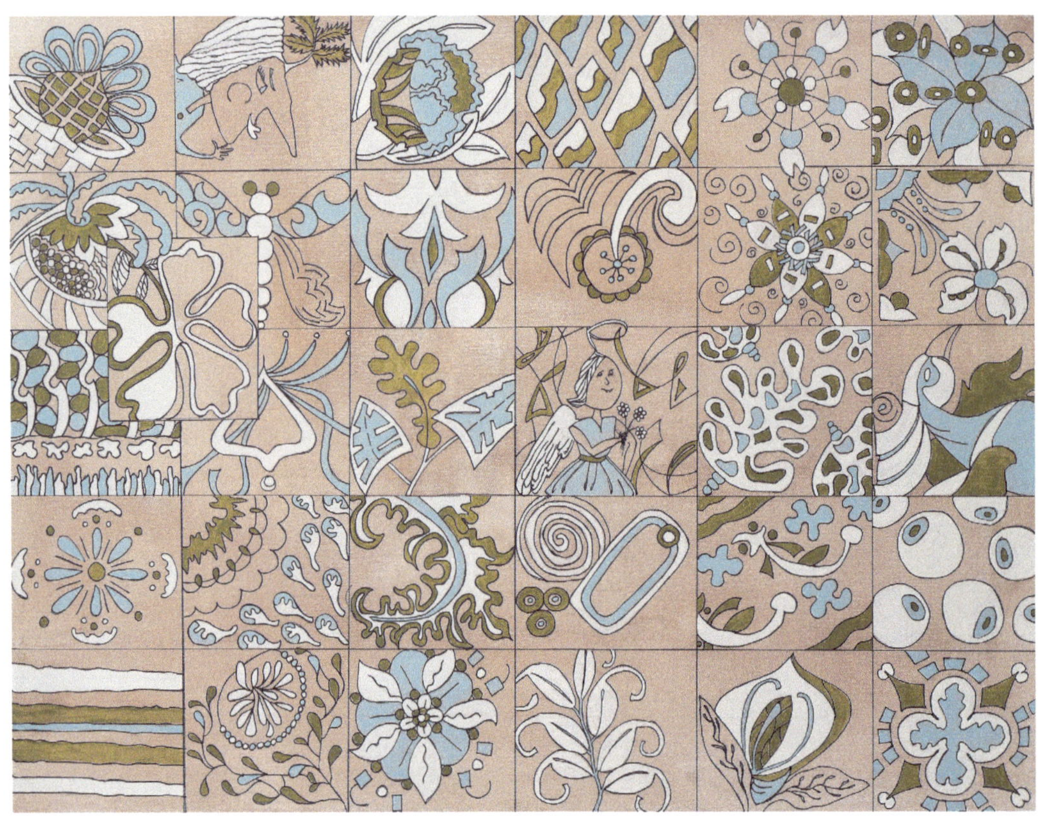

NO 14 : May 2009

PRAYER, THE FIRST STEP

My thoughts are focused on creative ideas. While they bounce around in my mind I muse on mentally sketching different scenarios of bringing these ideas to fruition. Looking for perspective I make a telephone call. By the eighth ring, panic hits and I become paralyzed by the startling thought that I cannot call my mom. My mom died.

The rude awakening deflated all enthusiasm, erasing the reason and the idea that prompted the call. Frantically grabbing for any thought, any memory, any moment of happiness, sadness, joy or sorrow that includes mom is a struggle. Unable to grasp a single one for my mind will not release the conclusive proof that I will never, ever be able to hear her voice or speak with my mom, ever again. The pain is gut wrenching.

I began to ponder my own death. In time it too will come and my being will fade from sight. My voice will also become bleached. Birth. Death. A transition. A new life without mom's voice. O, what will rescue my dismal spirit? Learning to live life without mom. How do I hush such an unsettling realization? Prayer, the first step.

If God wants to save us, nothing can kill us. If God wants to take us, nothing can save us.

Vedic Saying

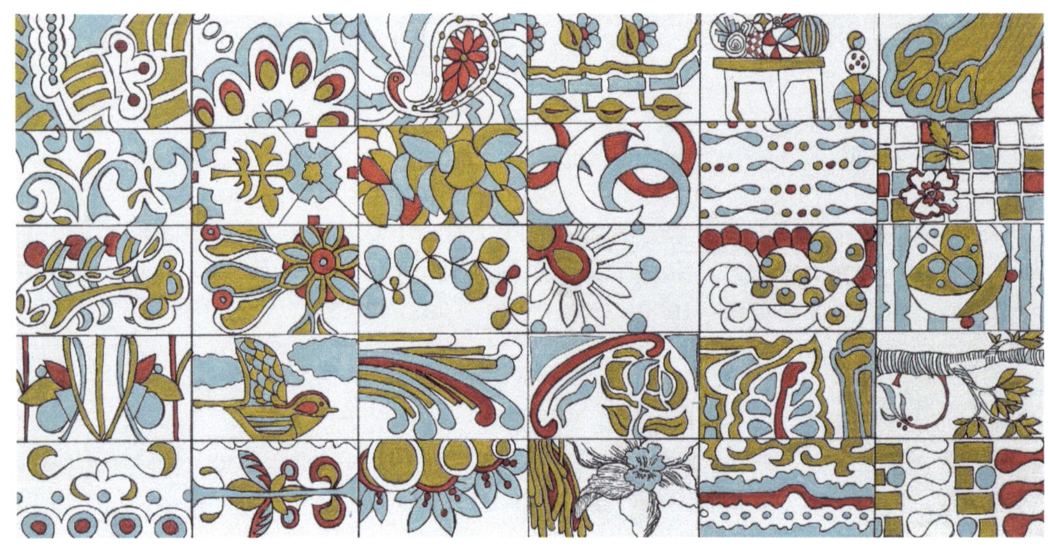

NO 15 : June 2009

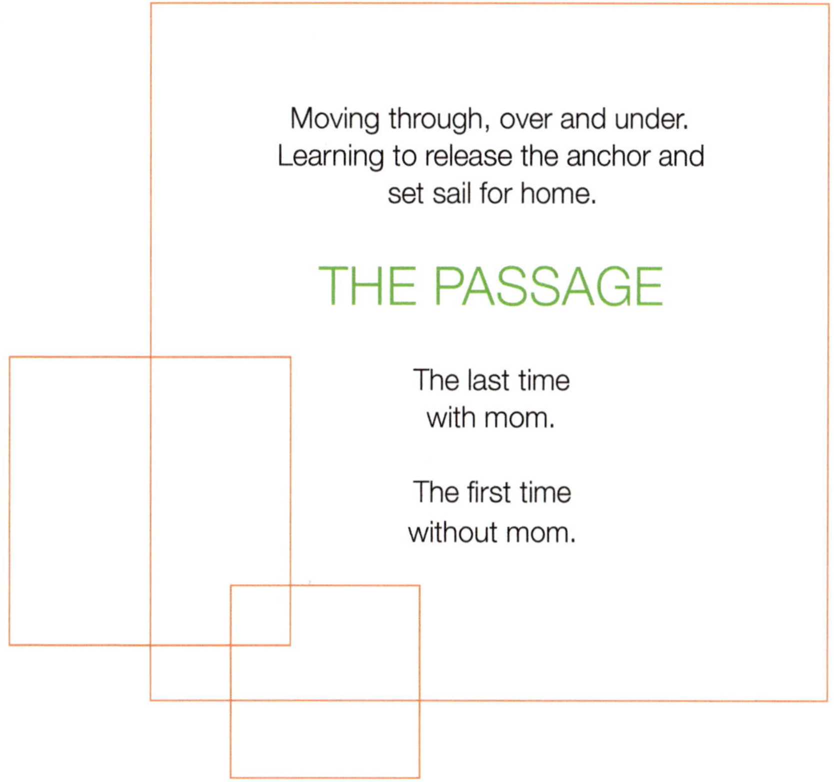

Moving through, over and under.
Learning to release the anchor and
set sail for home.

THE PASSAGE

The last time
with mom.

The first time
without mom.

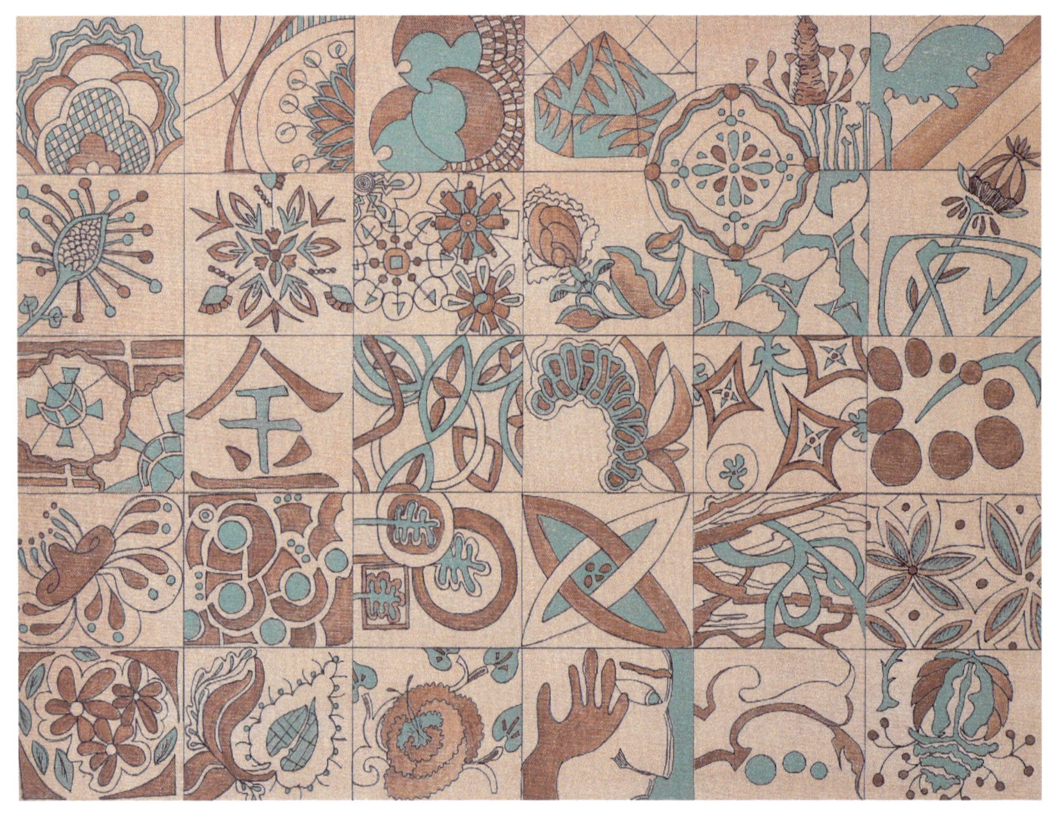

NO 16 : July 2009

GRIEF IS ONLY A VISITOR

When the memories surface, I watch with great intent. I welcome the reenactment, greet it with a smile while thoughts circulate the making of that memory.

Tears get in the way. Sometimes I shed a few, sometimes I shed many. Emotions need to run their course and the soul needs an occasional cleansing. Tears are an excellent way to revive the soul, renew a saddened spirit.

A hug helps too. I give the memories time to play from beginning to end; enjoying every emotion that occurred while making them. No matter how happy or sad, I often replay the memory by giving these ‘reminder moments’ the acknowledgment or praise they so deserve.

Grief is only a visitor. At times it lingers longer than I anticipated, though it is always treated with respect.

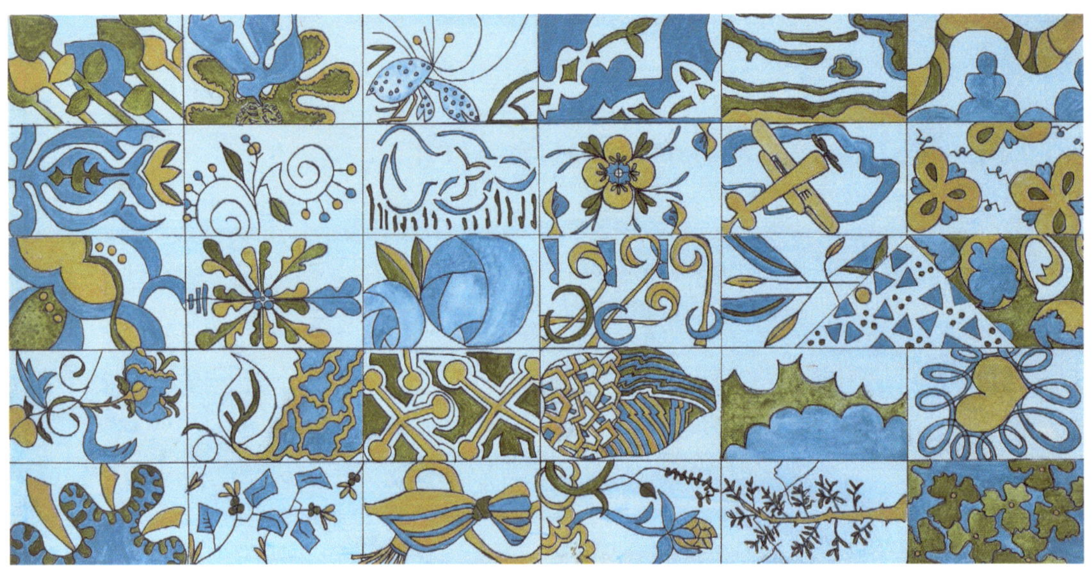

NO 17 : August 2009

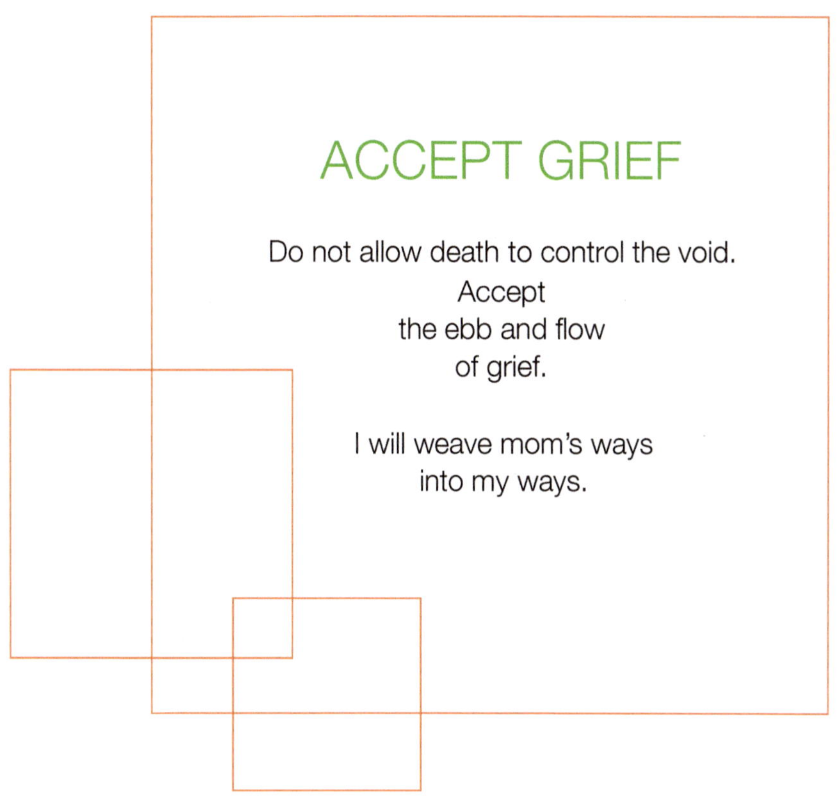

ACCEPT GRIEF

Do not allow death to control the void.
Accept
the ebb and flow
of grief.

I will weave mom's ways
into my ways.

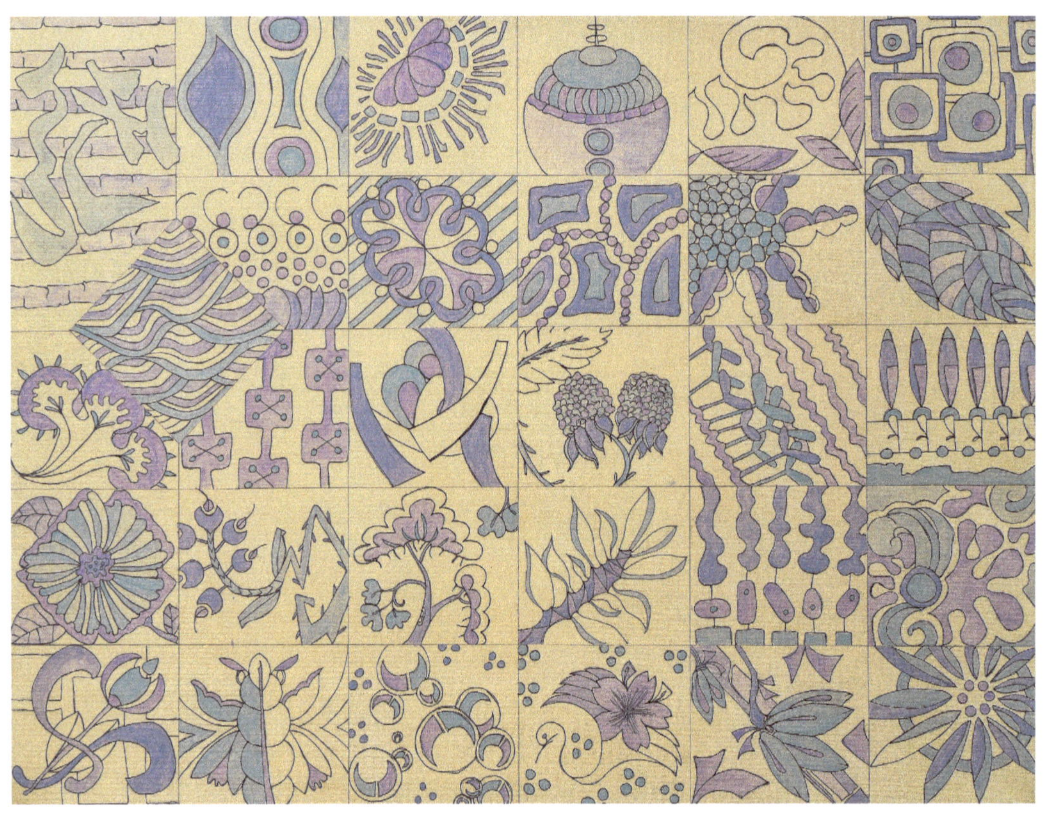

NO 18 : September 2009

TRUST

My days have not gotten any easier nor have they gotten any brighter. My spirit remains low and the cloud of gloom presses on, hovering even on the sunniest of days. The waft of illness and death continues to linger, to muddle. Six months since death found my mother and still, I am unable to focus and slow to make decisions, restless and inattentive. Blessed with another day despite the difficulty to sometimes carry on I convince myself that I am OK, and really I am, aren't I?

I think of my sister who lives in Washington State and my brother who lives in Texas. I wonder how different grief is when one is far away from the life and times of one who dies, compared to the grief when one is within hands reach of the life and times of one who dies. Is the pain any more or any less? As one grieves is it more helpful to be far away or within reach?

Sometimes my brain is humming a hive of activity and it never seems to hush. My memory is flooded with the laughter, the tears, the lively personality, the song and dance, the hugs, the will, the ways of mom bringing comfort to my discomfort. Sometimes the memories of mom are not enough to ease my pain. Sometimes I need, I want the sheer beauty of my sister and brother's presence, to be surrounded by their mosaic pieces of self, those colorful and not so colorful. I patiently await for their return, for where they are, mom is. The closest I can get to mom is being in their company. Whether I get what I need or what I want, I trust that it brings solace and hope.

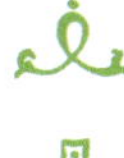

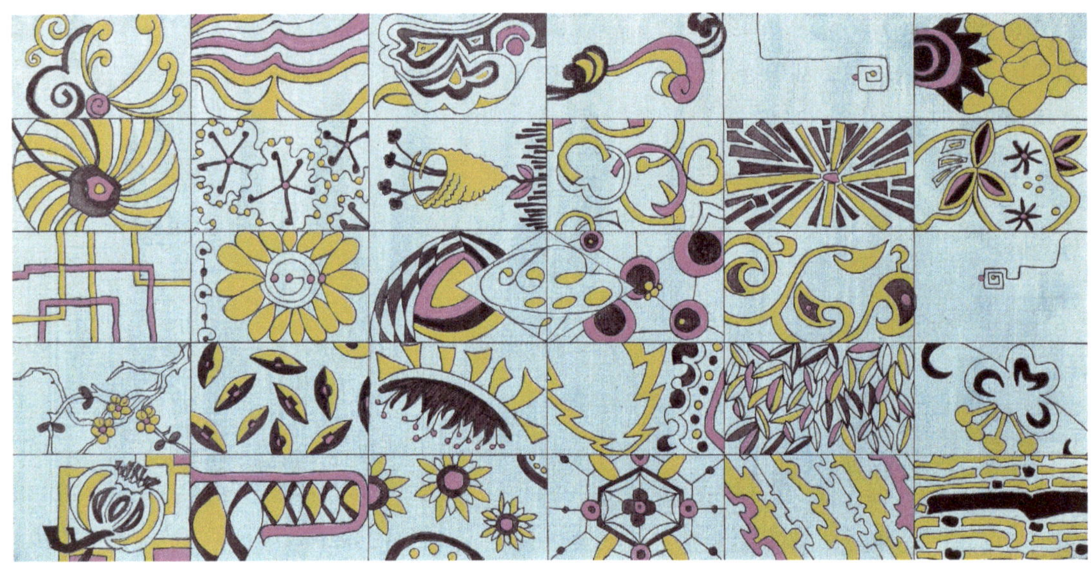

NO 19 : October 2009

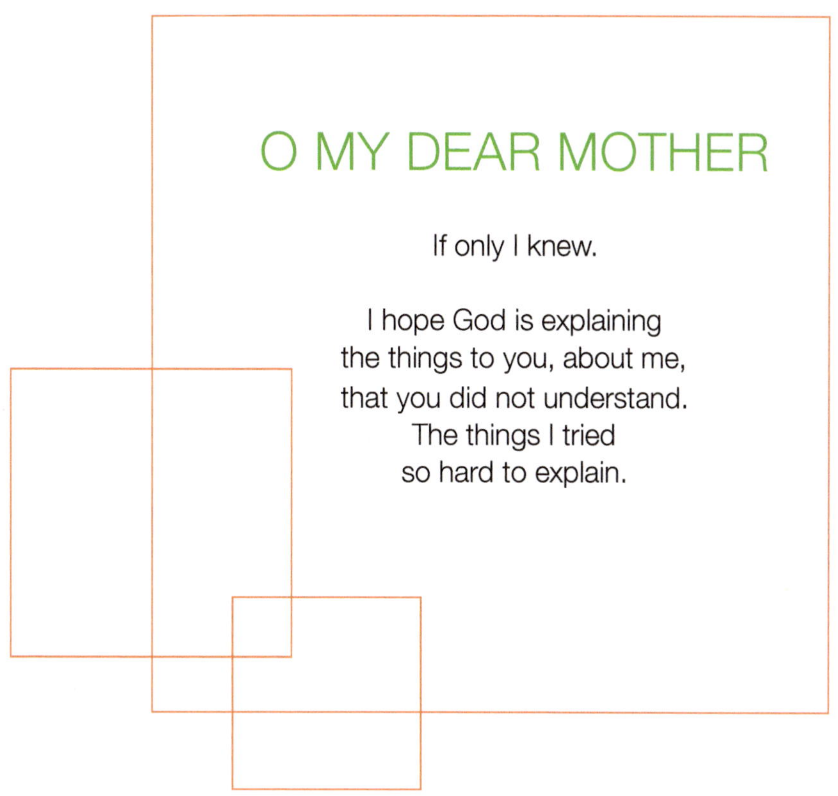

O MY DEAR MOTHER

If only I knew.

I hope God is explaining
the things to you, about me,
that you did not understand.
The things I tried
so hard to explain.

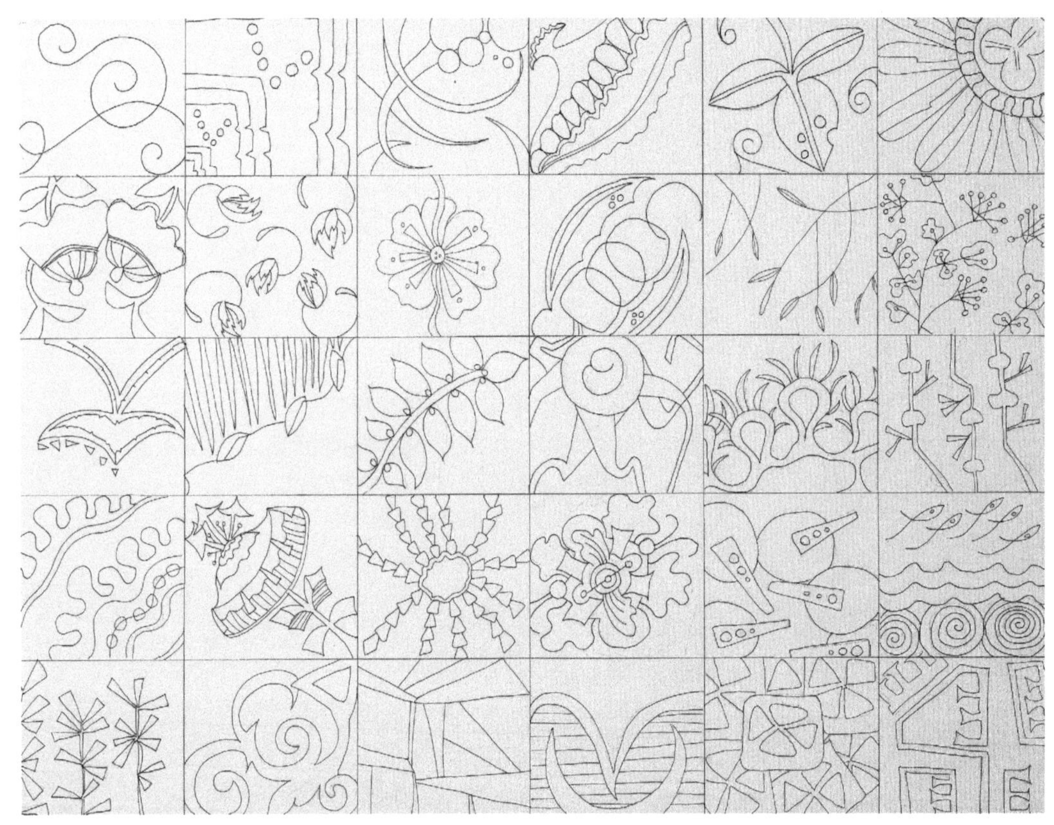

NO 20 : November 2009

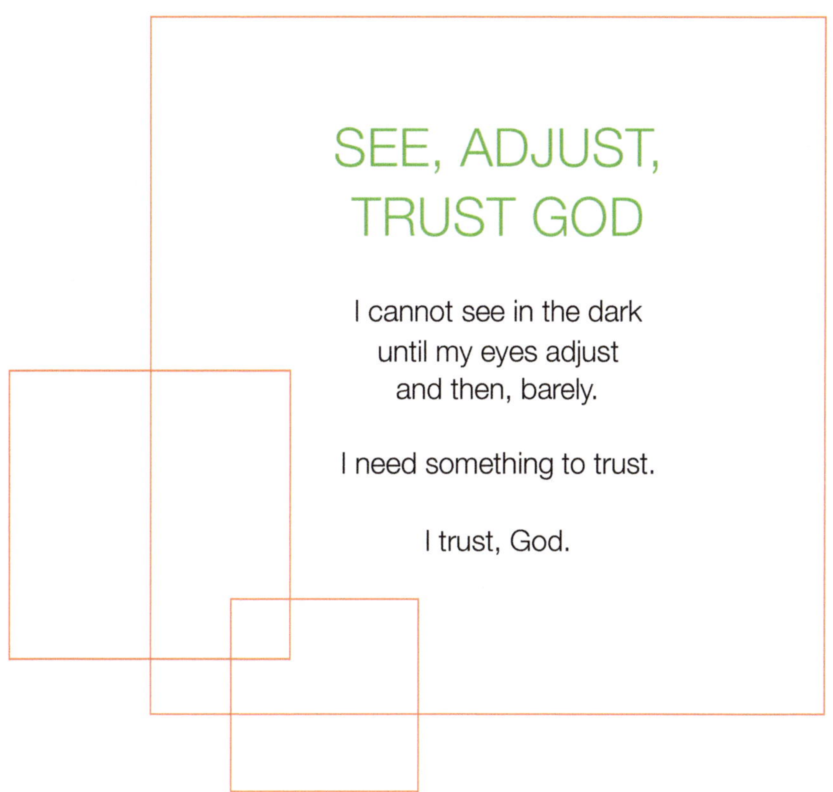

SEE, ADJUST, TRUST GOD

I cannot see in the dark
until my eyes adjust
and then, barely.

I need something to trust.

I trust, God.

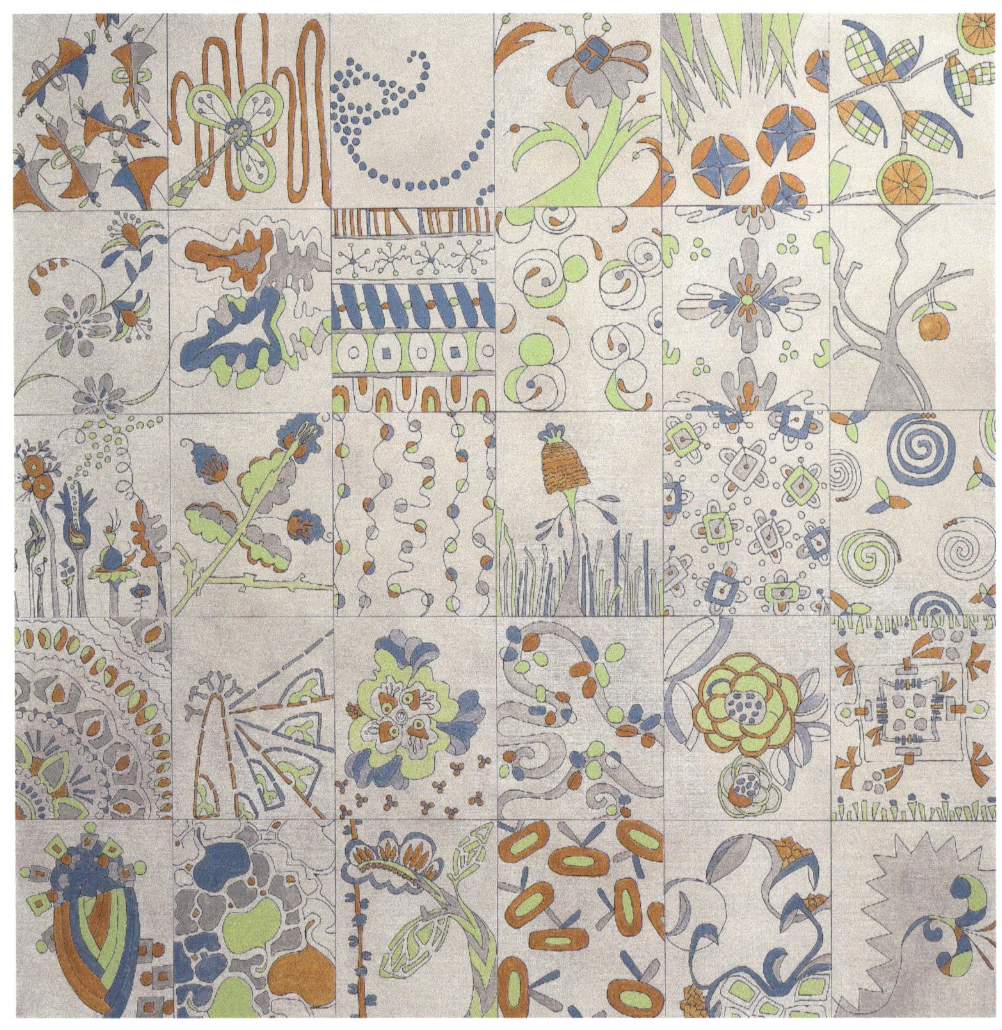

NO 23 : April 2011

COMMITMENT, ACCEPTANCE, CHANGE

Making the commitment to fix what is wrong
according to my interpretation is useless until acceptance of death's reality.

Yesterday, today, tomorrow still comes no matter what.

I cannot change my feelings or my actions until my mind is ready.

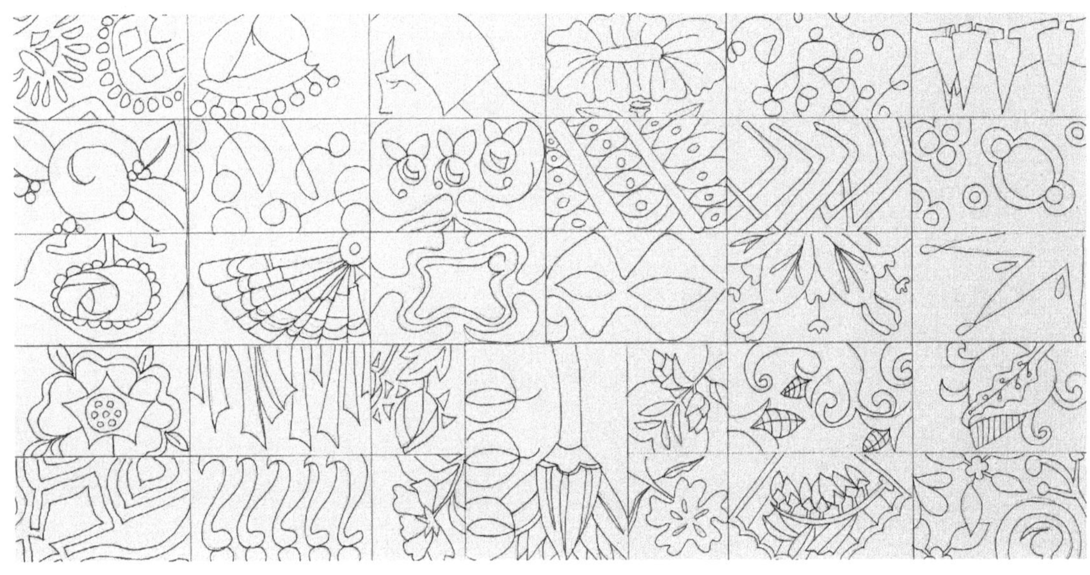

NO 21 : December 2009

In the crosswinds and perils of death I search for what provides stability and direction. Sometimes the quietude with self is the best approach for healing. There are no platitudes, no attitudes or no, “you should have.”

AND THEN

Clouds scud across the blue sky claimed by the wind.
Bluejays, non-stop in their attempt to entertain? To warn?

Wind chimes resonate from one corner of the garden
to a tune most pleasing to the ear
despite the excruciating headache
and heartache of sadness.

Morning sun warms the body as quickly as the wind cools

and then
a shift of wind silences.

Wind chimes no longer chime,
the bluejay melody concludes, clouds pass from sight.
The mind reconciles.

Always changing… something is.

Not lost our beloved but a cloud
manifesting in a different form.

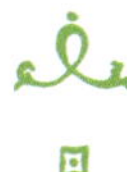

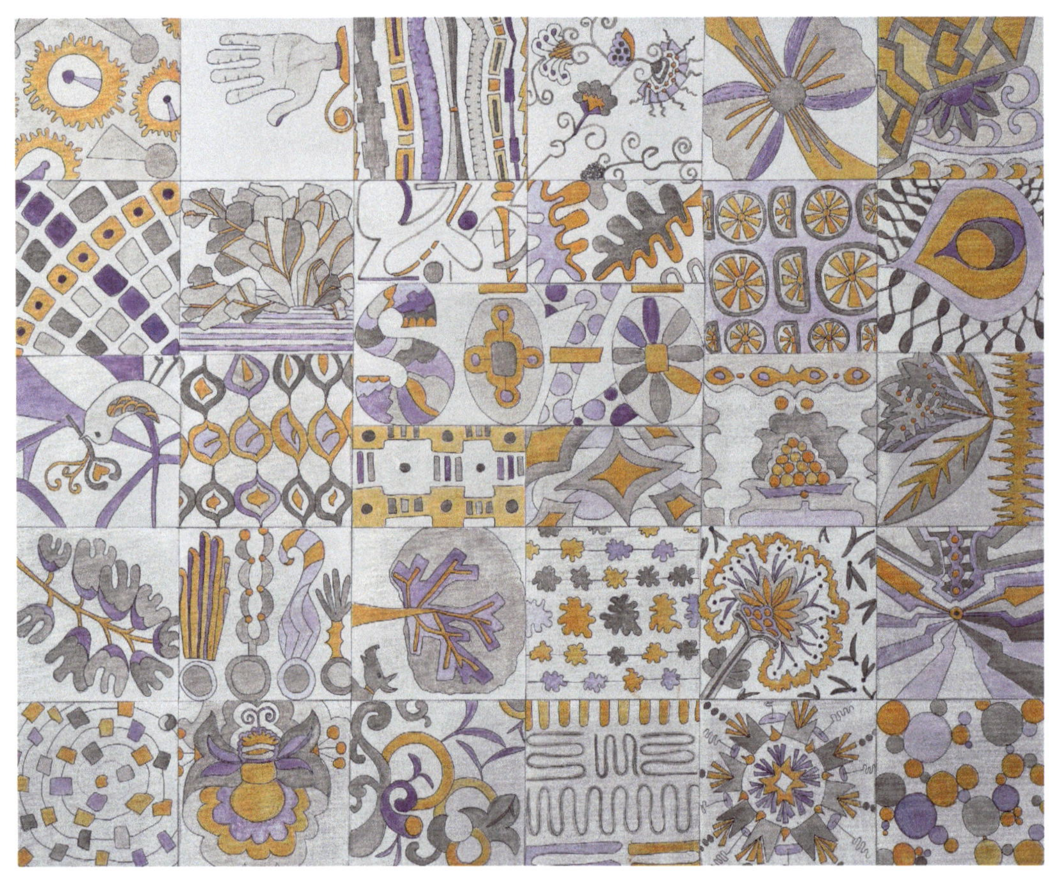

NO 25 : August 2012

TO ENDURE IS HEALING

I spread a sheet in the front yard on this day allowing the winter sun to blanket me in warmth, providing the perfect comfort from the cool afternoon breeze. Laying on my back I am entertained by the stark blue sky, the rustling of tree branches as they dance to the rhythm of the wind, watching with intent as an occasional leaf loses its place on a branch and billowing gracefully to the ground. I think of nothing but God, heaven and my mom.

How can I see, hear and touch the beauty of life she left behind if I am too busy wallowing in my sorrow? How can I honor her wishes if I focus on searching for something that is ultimately unknown?

Mesmerized by the beauty of nature, I realize how I handle death will either make or break me. Such will determine the quality of the rest of my life. It is my duty to honor my mom and continue with life as she had asked me to do. The spirit of my faith wraps my soul in comfort giving me the strength to endure the sadness that resides, temporarily. Patiently I must wait for the renewal of life. My faith has made me well. Until then, it is there in the comfort, love and support from family, friends and strangers that will lead me back to the road of healing grace.

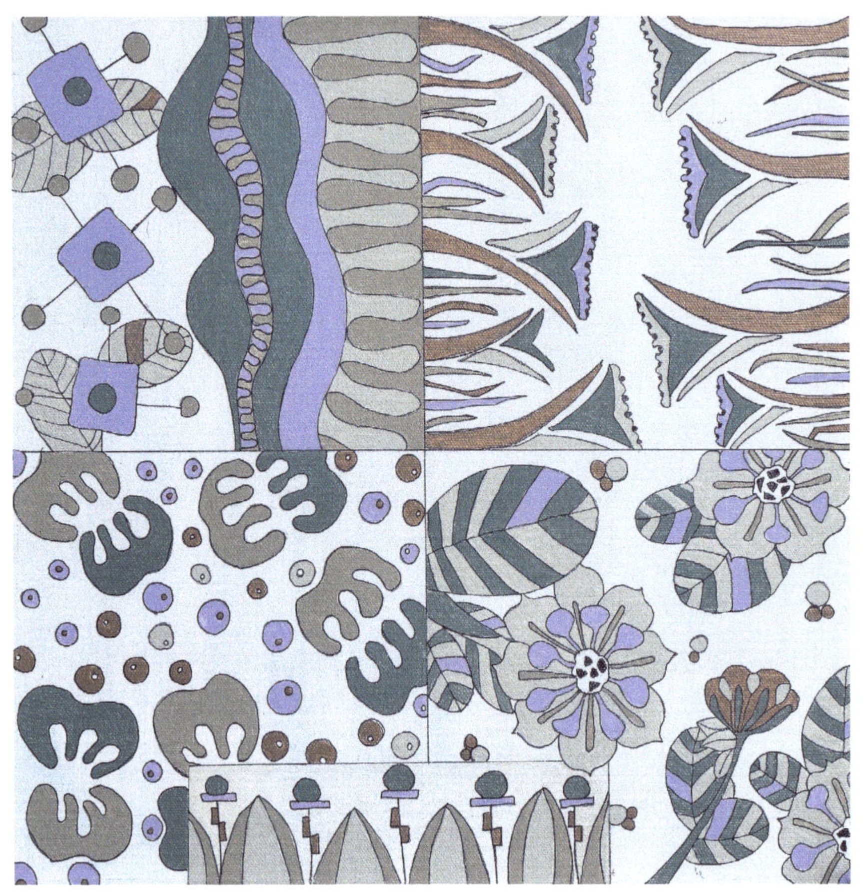

NO 27 : December 2012

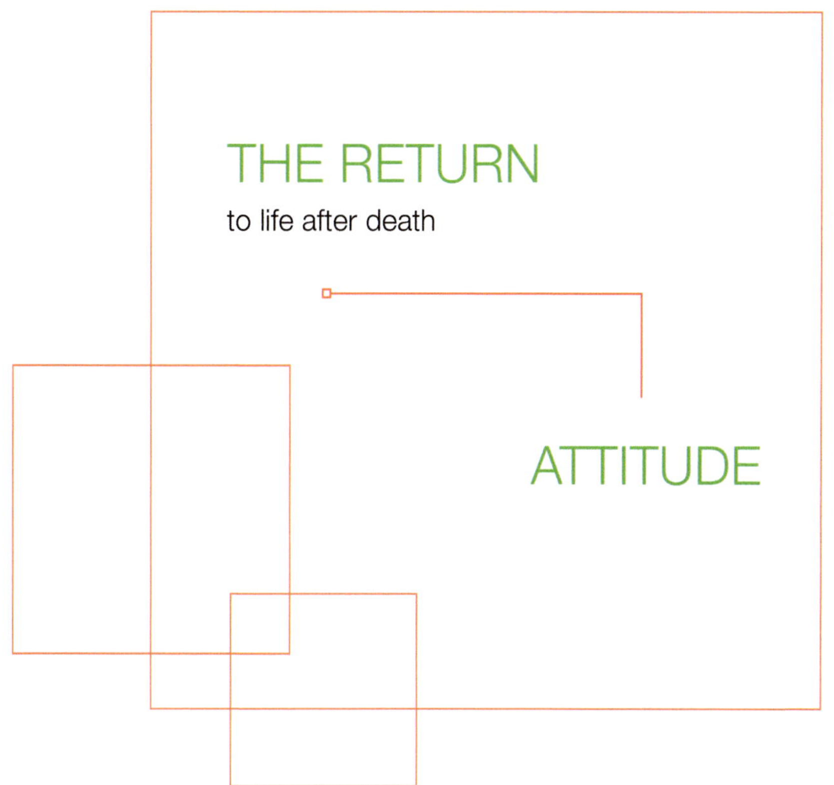

THE RETURN

to life after death

ATTITUDE

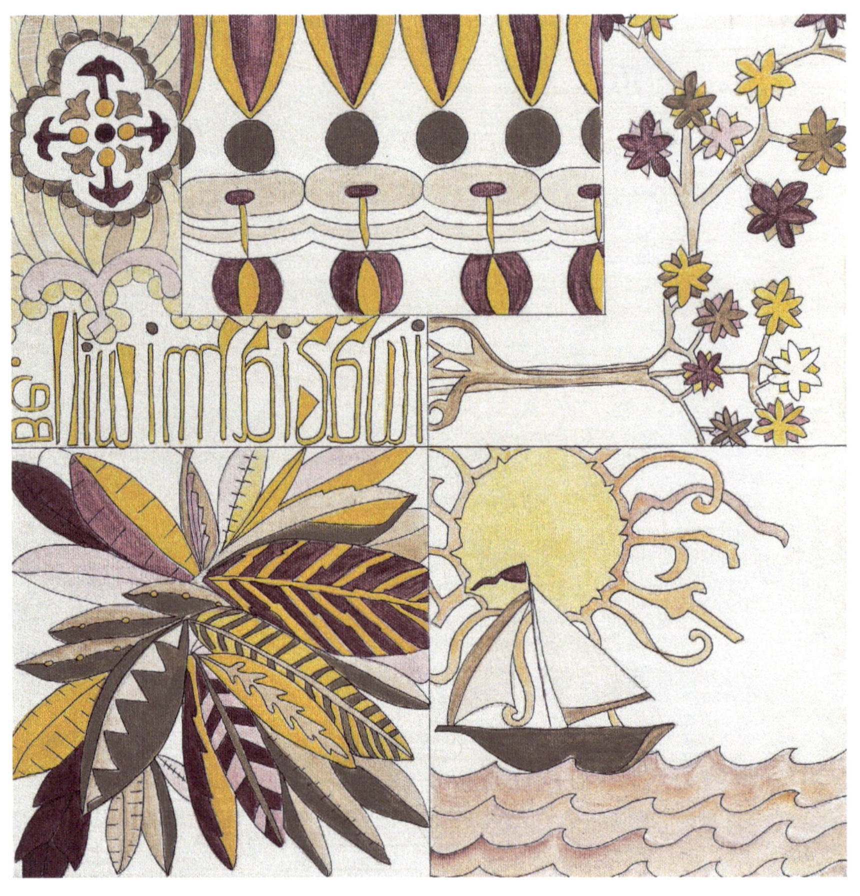

NO 28 : January 2013

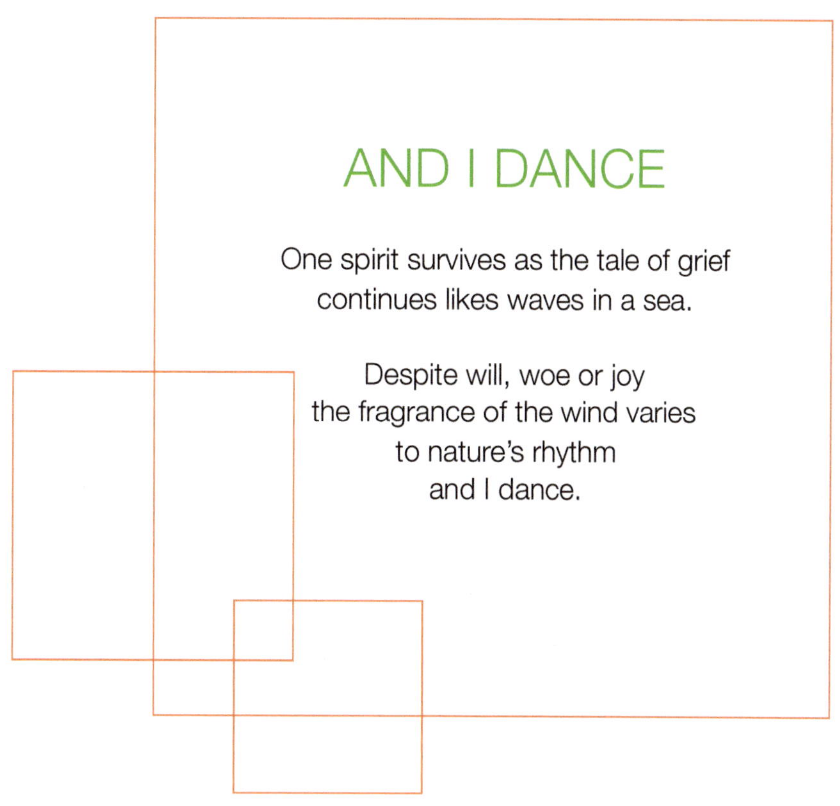

AND I DANCE

One spirit survives as the tale of grief
continues likes waves in a sea.

Despite will, woe or joy
the fragrance of the wind varies
to nature's rhythm
and I dance.

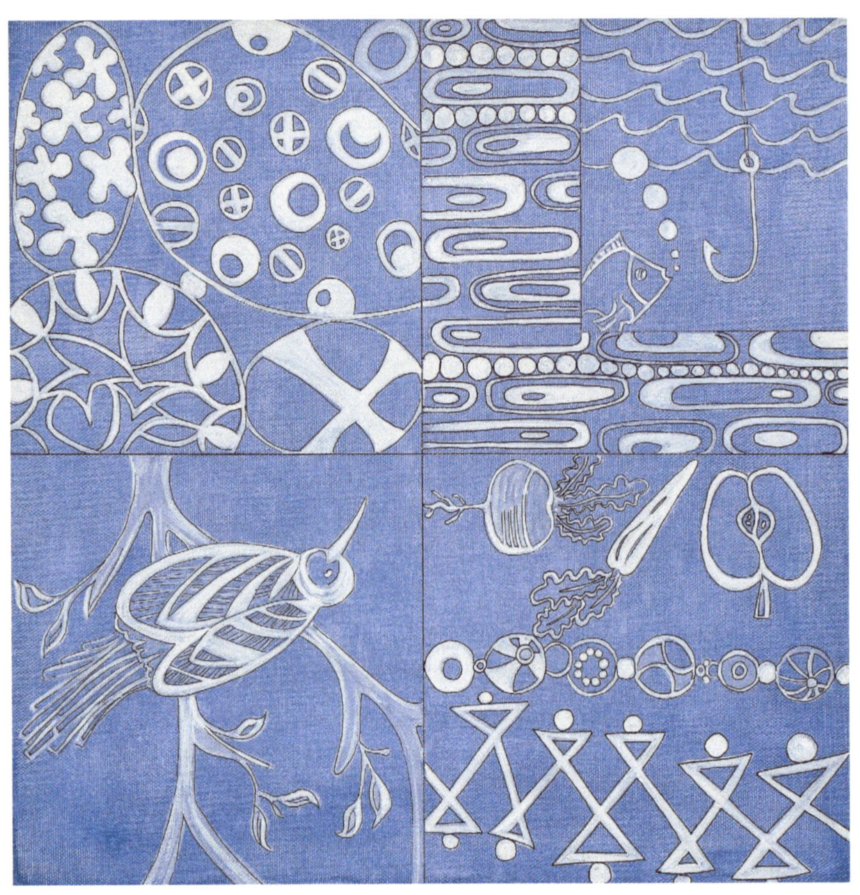

NO 35 : April 2014

RITUALS AND TRADITIONS

Aside, though not dismissing my spirituality and faith, my personal belief in Jesus Christ as Lord and Savior, I remain intrigued by rituals and traditions of other faiths and worship. As I continue to restore harmony in my mind and my life after mom's death, I remove myself from my norm and venture.

Obon is an annual Buddhist event commemorating one's ancestors. Praying for the repose of souls for their spirit to return to their homes, to reunite with family. Customs vary from region to region and take place typically in July. The difference and the contrast between similar circumstances or situations, people or cultures allow me to awaken further from the shadows of grief and death.

Rituals and tradition, I create my own Obon. Debra's style. Annually, on January 12th I remember, celebrate and honor my mother with the following:

OBON

- Gather a photo(s) of mom.
- Light a candle for the solemnity of the occasion.
- Prayer/reflection directed to the source from which I draw my spiritual strength.
- Wear, touch or hold if even for a brief moment, a personal possession of my mom's.
- Do something mom enjoyed, visit a place she visited or where we were together.
- Dine at one of mom's favorite spots or cook one of her favorite recipes.
- Make a toast to mom and to life, enjoying her favorite cocktail, Mango Madness.
- Plant a plant (mom, being a master gardener, I continue her passion).
- Pray for others who died or those who are in the process of with strength and healing to their family.

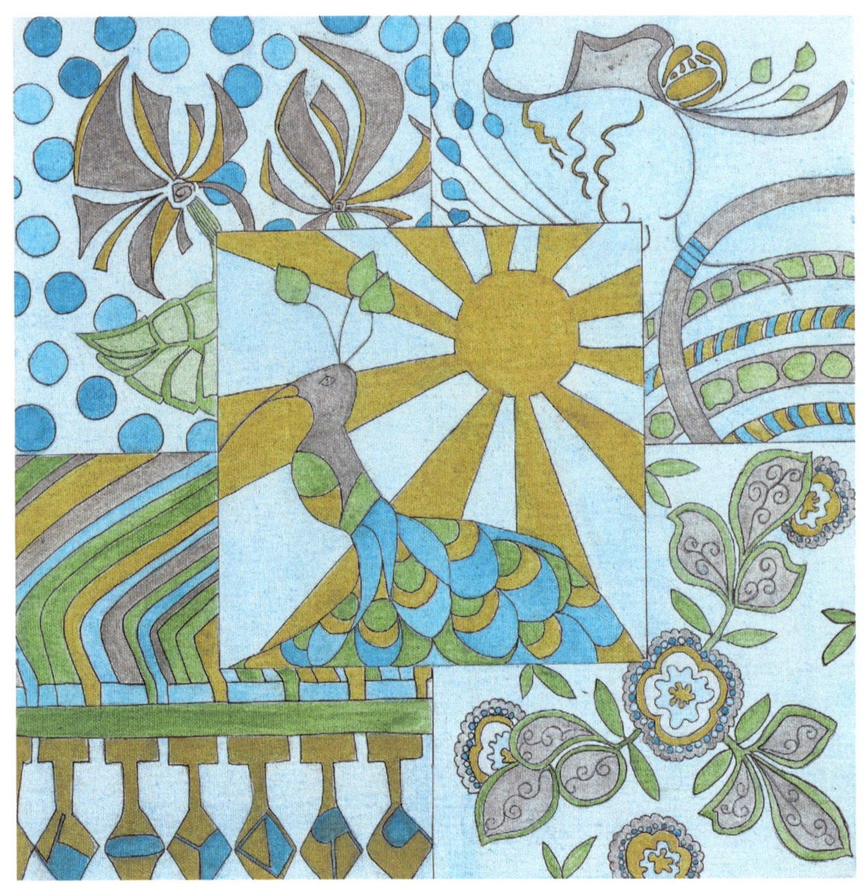

NO 30 : March 2013

Crossing the bridge from grief to healing.

FOUND SOLACE

Attainment of survival
new day, every day
life with a void
I must abide.

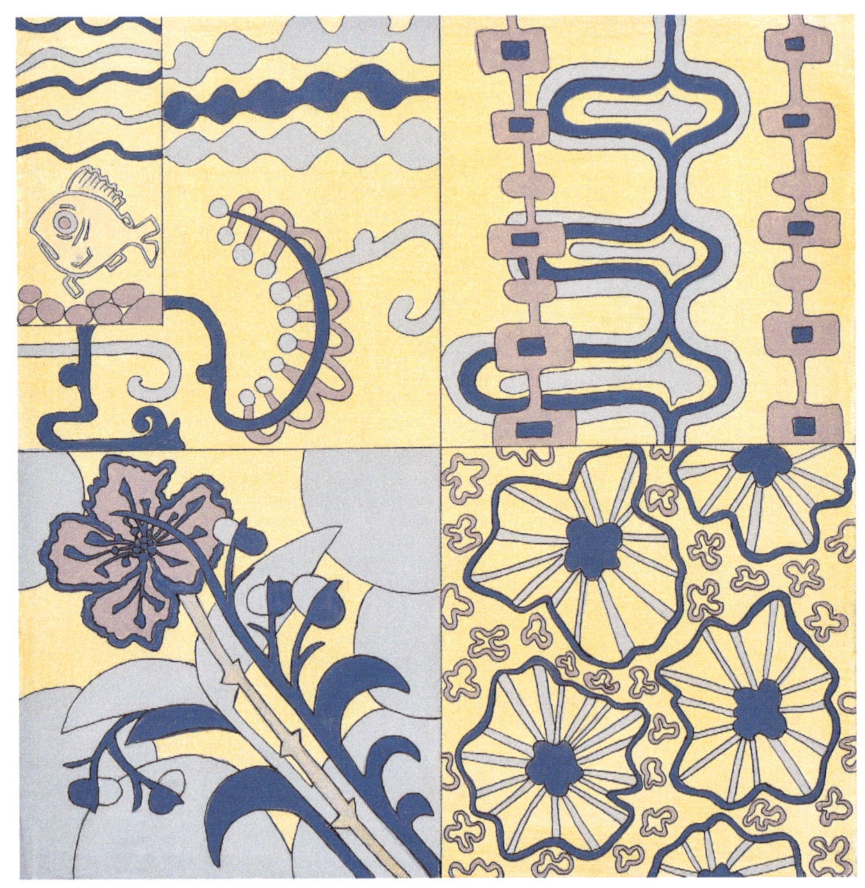

NO 36 : May 2014

EPILOGUE

In the sadness and pain from loss we experience a roller coaster of emotions usually offering a futile attempt to move through our grief. At some point we become a resident in a community where we are isolated and not necessarily due to our choice. When that happens, we need to realize that sometimes all we have to help us heal is within ourselves. To heal from the sadness, in a time and in a way that works for us.

Our brain is not working as we know it so making a commitment to restore harmony to our life after loss can be the hardest thing to do. Especially when family and friends no longer acknowledge or inquire and support resources exhausted. The second hardest thing to do is muster up the energy to venture out. To find alternative ways to help wade through your grief by yourself and for yourself. Doing so may lead to or even allow closure to your grief. Grief varies greatly from person to person in its intensity, length and effect. There is no right way or wrong way. Remember it is your sadness, your pain, your grief. Take the time and methods that work for no one but you.

When I dared to look outside the box of my standards, opening my eyes to see beyond my own understanding and expectation I learned to step away from my grief. I began to observe others in their grief and I decided to allow pain and sadness to be my teacher. It entailed making discoveries that were often more scary, worrisome and fearful then not. During the experience, how I handle, cope and deal is what will ultimately determine the quality of my life after loss.

When support systems no longer provided the support I wanted or needed, I found what worked for me, according to my time. I began by accepting the loss and befriended grief leading me to, Tending To My Wounds, Coping with Grief One Square at a Time and what became the final steps to my journey through loss, putting closure on my grief.

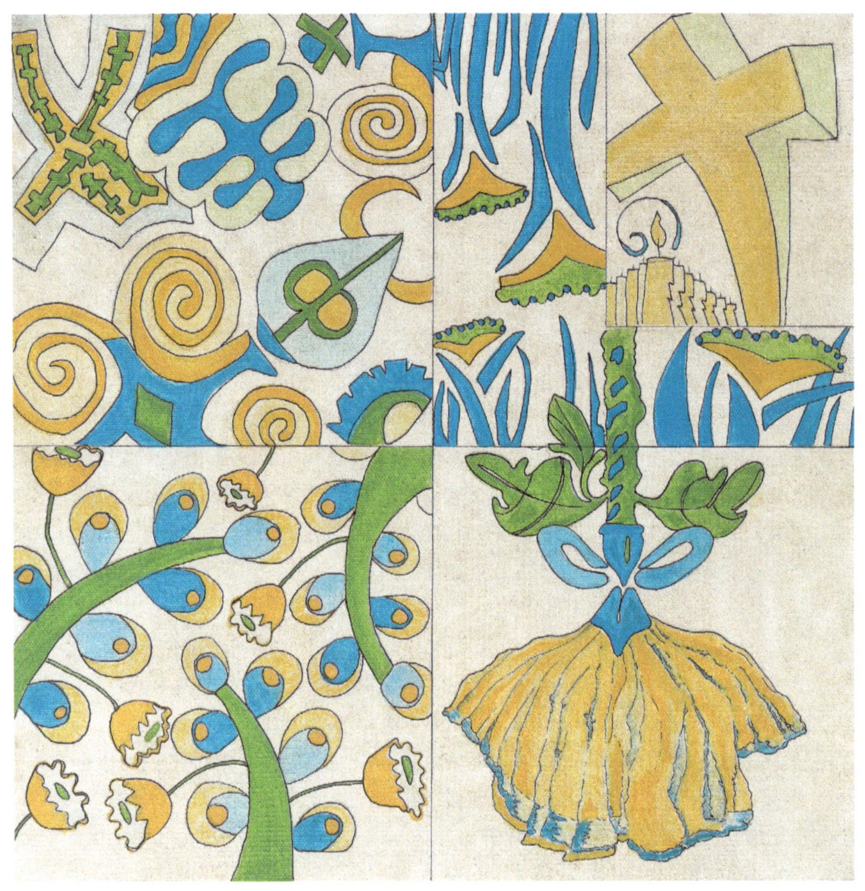

NO 29 : February 2013

I am different now. Those I know may or may not have noticed, yet I can tell. Grief is no longer painful. Although the sadness of my mother's death will always linger within my heart and soul, with adjustments I was able to regain harmony to and momentum in my life — you can too — in your own way, your own time. The grief, the sadness you experience is yours, do not feel guilty to treat it and yourself kindly. That may be your deliverance.

Thank you for viewing my art and journal entries. Perhaps this book offered some insight, acted as a guide to liberation or helped to encourage you on your own path to recovery. Being creative can be a great benefit in the healing process, so whether you decided to create your own square-a-day or found a different method to create I would be honored to hear, to see your discoveries. Contact me at www.dswalling.com.

Peace, Happiness, Love

CANVAS ANNOTATION

The Portrayal of My Grief (as shown on page 15) explains how I approach each square. What fills each square on all the canvases is based on that premise. There is no order to how the days of the month line up. I randomly pick a square and allow the hand to fill the space. What to draw? Some days I had a specific focus, some days not. Either way I kept within the time allowed, each day, each square. The following annotation lists my mindset for this particular canvas. If no annotation is given for a particular square it was created without preconceived thought.

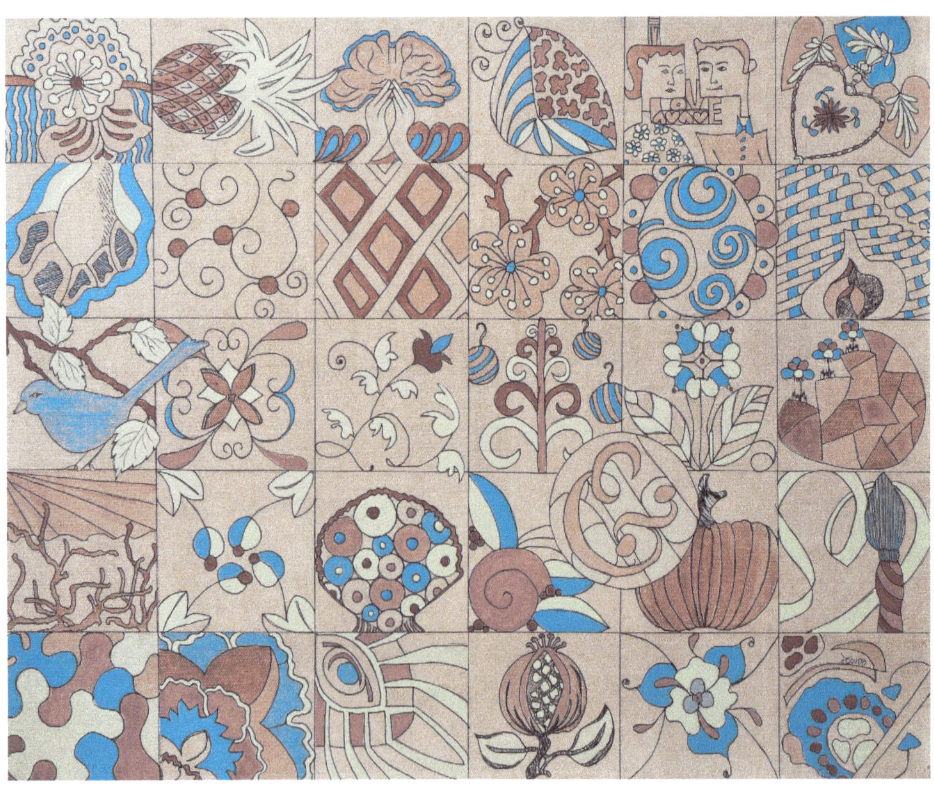

From left to right :

TOP ROW

pineapple: Feeling hospitable; possibly attempt to socialize/entertain.

folded hands: Sometimes prayer is the only answer.

female/male: Commitments to birth, death; to sadness, happiness. Commitment on this day, 17th wedding anniversary to Jeffrey.

heart: Lost keyring during our family trauma, a gift from my mom. Found on this day, two years after her death, in her car.

2RD ROW My mind would think one thought and the hand created something completely different. No reason, just because.

3RD ROW

bird: While outside, listening to a bird's trill.

tree: Unrewarding thoughts; first Christmas without mom. Thinking of my sister, my brother and myself (the 3 floating bulbs). I wonder how we will choose to survive the holiday. Together or alone.

cracked egg: My sister, brother and I (the 3 flowers) I think how differently we grieve. We all walk on eggshells; they don't want to talk about it.

4TH ROW

circles: Admiring the beauty of a scallop shell; my attempt to draw was obviously a failure.

and/ampersand: Thinking… and where did my family and friends go?

5TH ROW

puzzle: Puzzles… poems… death too can bemuse.

eye: Deliberate concealment — a mask to hide behind, no visitors please.

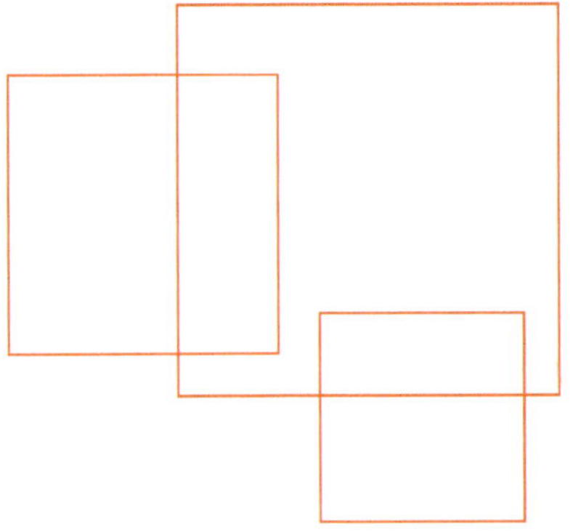

Healing from grief is not the process of forgetting,
it is the process of remembering with
less pain and more joy.

Author Unknown

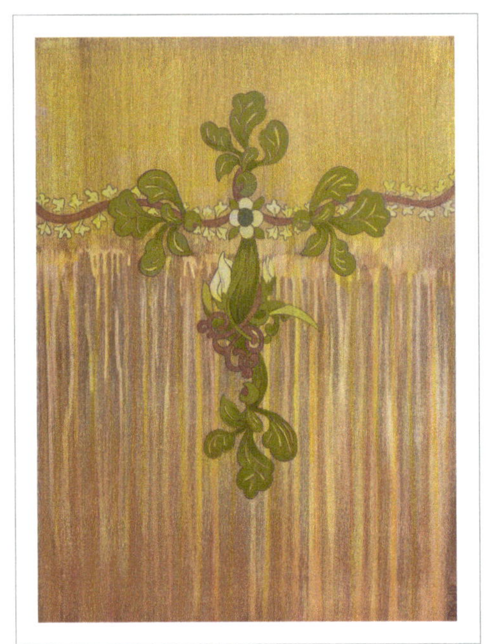

Thank You Jesus

www.ingramcontent.com/pod-product-compliance
Lightning Source LLC
LaVergne TN
LVHW070217110826
845147LV00003B/597

* 9 7 8 0 9 9 6 2 0 1 0 4 9 *